Collins

ENRICHING ENGLISH
Pedagogy with heart

A practical guide for new English teachers

Eleanor White

William Collins' dream of knowledge for all began with the publication of his first book in 1819.

A self-educated mill worker, he not only enriched millions of lives, but also founded a flourishing publishing house. Today, staying true to this spirit, Collins books are packed with inspiration, innovation and practical expertise. They place you at the centre of a world of possibility and give you exactly what you need to explore it.

Collins. Freedom to teach

Published by Collins
An imprint of HarperCollins*Publishers*
The News Building
1 London Bridge Street
London
SE1 9GF
UK

HarperCollins*Publishers*
Macken House,
39/40 Mayor Street Upper,
Dublin 1,
D01 C9W8,
Ireland

Browse the complete Collins catalogue at
collins.co.uk

© HarperCollins*Publishers* Limited 2024

10 9 8 7 6 5 4 3 2 1

ISBN 978-0-00-864091-0

British Library Cataloguing-in-Publication Data
A catalogue record for this publication is available from the British Library.

At the time of publication, the publishers acknowledge that sites and hyperlinks were verified and bear no responsibility for any subsequent URL domain change.

Author: Eleanor White
Publisher: Katie Sergeant
Product manager: Cathy Martin
Product developer: Saaleh Patel
Development editors: Marian Olney and Sonya Newland
Copyeditor: Jo Kemp
Proofreader: Catherine Dakin
Cover designer: Amparo Barrera, Kneath Associates
Internal designer and typesetter: 2Hoots Publishing Services Ltd
Production controller: Alhady Ali

Printed and bound in India by Replika Press Pvt. Ltd.

Contents

Chapter 1: The power of pedagogy

What does it mean to be an English teacher?

It is a real privilege to be an English teacher. This is a subject in which it is possible for students not only to achieve academic success, but also to develop personally, as it offers a unique opportunity to enhance empathy. English can also be a transformative subject, turning students into critics, poets, writers and readers by exploring an eclectic range of fiction and non-fiction texts. And this transformation may last far beyond the lessons you share with them. In the years to come, you will undoubtedly hear from students who have felt this transformation in significant ways in their life – by becoming an English teacher, for example!

English is a deeply human subject. Through English, we connect with writers and their world views; we connect with characters and their stories; we connect with one another through discussion. As such, it is important to keep the heart of the subject beating and ensure that pedagogy does not lose its soul by becoming too drenched in theory. The aim of this book is to help you deliver effective and engaging English lessons, instilling in your students a love for the subject, while keeping your own love for it alive.

The word 'pedagogue' dates back to ancient Greece, and refers to guides who would accompany wealthy students to school. You could see the pedagogies outlined in this book as guides to use throughout your English instruction. They are designed as frameworks, or schemas, to support you in teaching **oracy**, reading and writing. Within these schemas are specific approaches to learning – informed by research – that will enhance the results you will see in your classroom.

Besides acquiring knowledge and skills, the essence of English is the adventure... the experience. English is such a joy to teach because it's about seeing meaning in and making connections to our own lives and experiences, as well as to the lives and experiences of people in different times and in different societies. It is therefore essential that students enjoy an authentic personal experience in English, both in reading texts and in creating them themselves. When I was at school, there were two Year 12 classes, packed with keen girls ready to pull apart *Persuasion* and *Oranges Are Not the Only Fruit*. It is a time I will never forget. Now, there are reports that the subject is not recruiting well at A Level. A number of reasons have been suggested for this. Some argue that the current GCSE format is to blame or that the focus of the curriculum is too narrow. It could be that there is too much focus on technicalities such as vocabulary and historical context, which can prevent students from simply immersing themselves in the literature. I didn't look up a word of *Hamlet* before diving in; instead, I was allowed to enjoy the adventure and experience a personal, authentic response.

This sense of adventure is key to success in English teaching. We need to ensure that students are not just learning the technicalities of language, memorising events and quotations, and recalling mnemonics for writing. They should also be engaging with a wide variety of texts from diverse authors, and learning to understand the benefits of studying English. These include fostering a sense of belonging, connecting with characters in literature and history, and developing skills in speech and writing. The GCSE curriculum may be prescribed but, as Jo Heathcote explains in *Curriculum with Soul,* the companion volume to this book, Key Stage 3 can be an opportunity for students to explore different issues and make links between different texts, as well as to hone their writing abilities.

English is the gateway to every other subject, giving students tools for accessing everything they learn at school. It gives them a voice, enabling them to make sense of the world around them and to understand their place in it, including tackling important issues such as social injustice. English also helps students relate to others, to craft their language and to communicate effectively what they think and feel. There is huge power in the medium of writing and beautiful solace to be found in reading. It's here that students can be critical, make judgements and explore different perspectives. It is our job to not only impart the knowledge and skills students need to achieve these outcomes, but also to empower them to tell their own stories, creating a safe space in which they can do so.

> **Reflection**
> - What made you become an English teacher?
> - What is your vision for your classroom?
> - What do you think makes English unique?

Types of knowledge

According to Shulman (1986), there are two elements to English teaching: subject knowledge and pedagogical knowledge. Pedagogical content knowledge (PCK) is particular to teachers and is based on how we link our pedagogical knowledge (what we know about teaching) to our subject-matter knowledge (what we know about what we teach). In this sense, PCK is unique in English. Pedagogical knowledge and subject-matter knowledge will work in tandem throughout your career as you develop into an experienced practitioner. However, to begin with, you may have a vast amount of subject knowledge, with a degree in English, but limited knowledge of the pedagogies that underpin great teaching. In this book, I hope to bring a bit more balance to that knowledge by introducing a number of research-informed approaches that you can follow up on using the References section at the back of the book. Together, these types of knowledge will help you teach with heart.

Subject and pedagogical knowledge overlap in many different ways. For example:

Subject knowledge	Pedagogical knowledge	Teaching with heart
Themes and ideas in A Christmas Carol.	Scaffolding the reading experience (Graves and Graves, 2003).	Introducing 'predict' activities before reading to set a focus for the reading, unearthing themes.

This book focuses on how various pedagogies can support and scaffold the extensive subject knowledge you already bring to the classroom.

Pedagogical schema for oracy, reading and writing

We can enliven the threads of English (knowledge, skills and adventure) through pedagogical schema for oracy, reading and writing – what the Education Endowment Foundation (EEF) refers to as 'the vital interconnected networks of background knowledge' (EEF, 2021). Schemas are an element of cognitive science principles that work in English. In this book, I will show you how to organise the content knowledge into a sequence to support **mental models** of how to teach the different parts of English most effectively. To do this, each of the three schemas in the book follows four key stages: initiate, develop, collaborate and reflect. The idea is that these will become ingrained into your teaching practice, allowing you to structure and sequence your teaching efficiently and effectively.

Oracy

Just as the ancient Greeks recited the story of *The Iliad* orally, we begin learning and communicating **dialogically**. For this reason, our first schema is for oracy. We start, as we do with reading and writing, by initiating ideas and engaging in oracy through active listening. Listening is a difficult – and sometimes overlooked – skill, and it is important that students learn to develop empathy through listening and to hear beyond literal meaning.

The pedagogical schema for oracy (explored in Chapter 3) is as follows:

Oracy	Engage	Contribute	Explore	Challenge	Concur	Reflect
	Hook students with explicit listening activities.	Set ground rules so that everyone can be involved.	Allow time for students to consider new material and apply reasoning.	Use questioning and cognitive conflict.	Seek agreement.	Use **metacognition** to explore what's been learned.

Once students are engaged, you need to ensure that all members of the group know how to contribute. Chapter 3 will help you to establish the ground rules for this. Once the parameters have been set, you can move on to exploring ideas through talk and applying reasoning to discussions. Next, it is essential to develop some **cognitive conflict** (Adey and Shayer, 2015), to challenge students to look at events or ideas from different perspectives – a practice that enhances cognition. Mercer (2008) argues that it is effective to reach some sort of consensus in talk, so the penultimate stage in the schema is 'concur'. Finally, by encouraging students to think metacognitively and to reflect on where their talk has taken them, they are much more likely to follow the same pattern successfully in the future.

Reading

Chapter 4 explores how you can structure reading lessons to support students' development from inferential to interpretative readings of a variety of texts, and instil a love of reading for pleasure.

Firstly, it is important to note the value of diversity. It is crucial to give your students the opportunity to read from a rich culture of texts. The choice of texts may not be within your sphere of influence at the moment, but one day it will be your job to select what your students read, so encourage them to read as many different voices as possible.

The pedagogical schema for reading (explored in Chapter 4) is as follows:

Reading	Predict	Respond and elaborate	Infer	Explore	Judge
	Set predictive activities on the text.	Ask questions to secure comprehension. Ask questions that get students thinking across and beyond the text.	Explore abstract ideas.	Make connections beyond the text.	Summarise understanding through evaluation.

Research for reading comes largely from Graves and Graves (2003) and the Scaffolded Reading Experience, in which you will think about activities before, during and after reading. I have extended that experience to include response and elaboration on reading, and inferential and interpretative responses. It is important to allow students to evaluate texts and make judgements at the end of the schema.

Writing

In the schema for writing, I have developed the ideas of Hayes (2006) and Gibbons (2002) in process and product writing. Gibbons advocates for a four-stage sequence for teaching writing, which I have embedded with the practice of creating authentic pieces through activities such as **free writing** and pre-writing (Elbow, 1995).

The pedagogical schema for writing (explored in Chapter 5) is as follows:

Writing	Spark	Define	Draft	Compare	Refine	Develop
	Set the focus for writing; elicit ideas.	Identify the audience; explore genre and text type.	Use scaffolds to support the initial writing stage.	Live model and compare to sentence-level examples.	Continue live modelling; revisit success.	Ask students to redraft after reflection; use metacognitive strategies.

You might consider the schemas as interweaving sequences, scaffolding the three strands. They could be merged in the following way, with reading and listening forming the basis for speaking and writing:

Oracy	Reading		Reading/ Oracy	Oracy/ Reading	Oracy/ Writing	Writing	Oracy/ Writing
Engage	**Predict**	**Respond/ elaborate**	**Explore/ challenge/ infer**	**Judge/ reflect**	**Spark/ define**	**Draft/ compare/ develop**	**Reflect**
Pre-reading		Whole texts	Short passages	Sentences	Short passage	Whole texts	Reflection

Adapted from Rose (2016)

You can select discrete parts of the schema for your lessons or follow the schema in its entirety for an oracy, reading or writing unit of work, but the best way to embed them is to follow the overlapping sequence above. All elements of English support one another to allow students to become creative writers, critical thinkers and illuminative communicators.

Cognitive science that works in English

Cognitive science principles are in vogue at the moment, and you will probably hear about them in your school. One of the elements of cognitive science that can be supported by the schemas in this book is cognitive load theory. Students take information from their environment into their working memory, but this has limited space and trying to cram too much information in it can cause them to feel overwhelmed and demoralised by learning (Willingham, 2009). Instead, we want this information to move into their long-term memory. To do this, it helps to 'chunk' information for students – for example, by separating the elements of text types and by making writing sequential.

In English, it is also useful to **interleave** information and use **spaced practice** to consolidate ideas in students' long-term memory. For instance, imagine you taught *Oliver Twist* to a class in Year 8. Those students are now in Year 10, studying *A Christmas Carol*. You can interleave some of the students' general historical knowledge of Victorian England to develop their understanding of the social context of the novel. This allows students to make links between concepts and ideas, building their mental models. Students should see information and practise new skills several times after the first conception, with spaced practice spanning weeks or months.

Developing students' ideas through elaboration is integrated into our schemas. Responding to students' ideas in a **dialogic** classroom with questions like *Why? How? What if?* can support their development of ideas and their ability to make links knowingly. This is covered more fully in Chapter 3.

Another element of cognitive science that really works for English is modelling. Using tangible examples of concepts in action will support students in understanding high-level ideas and abstract meanings. Modelling is covered in all three of the schemas in the following chapters and is one of the main principles for effective teaching explored in Chapter 2.

Retrieval in English

Retrieval practice in English differs from subjects in which **declarative knowledge** is key. Retrieval in English is often based on remembering quotations. It's very difficult to use **retrieval practice** to assess students' wider knowledge of a text because we don't read in a vacuum. A reader's response to a text comes from different forms of knowledge – an interconnected web of ideas that can be difficult to define through five questions at the start of the lesson. How a reader feels about the character of Juliet may depend on a poem or non-fiction article they have previously read, a personal experience, or some news from their local area. Similarly, students might know what a metaphor is, but they need exposure to metaphor in a variety of contexts to really understand the impact of this type of figurative language. And this, of course, is difficult to quantify through a recall question. This is why students' experience of English is enriched by varied exposure.

As a teacher, I loved reading poetry with students, delving into plays, looking at theatrical representations, exploring different examples of one writing genre, reading different non-fiction articles on topics that inspire young people. This is the kind of exposure we want for students in the English classroom, but it's difficult to quantify, as we can't test its impact. In English, we are looking to develop knowledge and skills while encouraging and enjoying a sense of adventure. This can come from starter activities in your scheme of work. There's no need to hammer home quotation retrieval; examiners are looking for 'textual references', which means demonstrating knowledge of the content of a text. This means that you can focus on helping students with the retrieval of ideas, and on making links across the text. Look at this example for *Othello*.

Start with a <u>responsive question</u> to the text (*Othello*):

1. What does 'Valiant Othello' suggest? (I.3)

Then set a <u>memory test with references</u> that will support learning:

2. Complete the sentence: She had _____ and chose _____ (III.3)

Now move on to an <u>elaborative exploration</u> of ideas:

3. Othello mentions his blackness, his unsophisticated manners and his age in Act III. What does this suggest about him?

Then think about <u>connection across the text itself</u>:

4. 'I will not kill thy unprepared spirit' (V.2). How does Othello feel about Desdemona now?

And finally ask a question that demands <u>connection within and across the text</u>:

5. How has Othello changed from the play's opening to Act V?

This sequence of questions gives students the opportunity for more of an adventure with the text. There may not be one perfect answer for each question for students to self-assess against, so instead, follow up these questions with a discussion – a dialogic approach (after all, pedagogy is historically thought of as a Socratic approach to teaching). Discussion validates students' perceptions and allows them to learn and develop by listening to others' ideas.

The three 'threads' of English

The focus of English teaching, then, can be divided into three key areas: knowledge, skills and adventure. Students' knowledge accumulates and develops over texts and over time. The text should be dominant here; background knowledge should be recognised but should not take centre stage. It's possible to read poetry or drama and still make sense of it without a history lesson. This approach is vital, as it allows the student to offer an authentic personal response.

In English, then, we teach three things:

What we teach	Examples	How we teach
What you know	What eclectic means; who Inspector Goole is; a quotation to suggest some kind of emotion.	Retrieval and spaced practice; 'pre-reading' activities; post-reading activities.
What you can do	Explore connotations; use a subordinate clause to add tension	Active reading; the writing schema; modelling.
How you feel	Solace from reading a poem; connection to a character or experience; the joy of the experience of reading *Animal Farm*	Demonstrating joy in teaching; giving students freedom; instilling the pleasure of making connections.

I would argue that how students feel – the adventure of English – takes precedence over what they know and what they can do (knowledge and skills), although it's difficult to know if we are teaching this well. However, the connection that students develop with a text or a piece of writing can keep them in English classrooms to A Level and beyond, so it's essential to focus on the adventure, so that students can access the subject and begin to love it. If you focus on the ideas in the text and the pleasure to be gained from reading it, recall of important references and quotations will naturally follow. You will also start to love your pedagogical practice more.

Planning

Planning should be an integral part of your practice. There are three planning phases:
- long term: over school years, probably already set by your department
- medium term: over half terms (you may do some of this planning this year)
- short term: individual and weekly plans.

Long-term planning marks the high-level goal for the unit of work; the objectives of this come from the curriculum. Medium-term planning – which you may do at some point this year – goes into further detail and is more precise about objectives and outcomes of each unit of work. This will allow you to sequence learning towards the high-level goal over a period of time. Short-term plans add more detail to daily/weekly lessons.

A worked example for English planning would be:

Long term	GCSE Language writing skills:				
	• Communicate clearly and effectively, organise ideas.				
	• Use a range of vocabulary and sentence structures, accurate spelling and punctuation.				
Medium term	Gothic writing: Focus on organisation of ideas and using a range of vocabulary.				
Short term	Story openings	Focus within paragraphs	Sentence-level development	Dynamic verbs in sentences	Extended writing practice

Task

Try planning a focus for five lessons with the high-level goal of developing analytical writing. Use the template below.

Long-term	GCSE Language reading skills:				
	• Identify implicit and explicit information in texts.				
	• Explain, comment on and analyse how writers use language and structure to achieve effects.				
	• Use subject terminology.				
Medium-term	Non-fiction texts: Focus on exploring effects of language, selecting judicious evidence and using subject terminology.				
Short-term					

When planning, it is important to avoid cognitive overload. You can do this by introducing new material in small, chunked steps. Use interleaving and sequence learning so students are recapping previously learnt material.

Always keep in mind the three parts of English: knowledge, skills and adventure. Aim to solidify declarative knowledge, give students time to practise skills, and bring in a playful element to English so young people feel part of the adventure of the subject.

The best plans go backwards

Starting at the end is one of Lemov's (2021) main principles, and backwards planning has long been a popular technique among English teachers. Think about the end of your lesson – what do you want your students to be able to do by the time they walk out of the classroom in an hour's time? Use these three questions to guide you:

- What do I want my students to do?
- How will I know they have done this well?
- What steps will I take to get them there?

You could use the following planning template to frame the lesson:

What do I want students to do? Driving question:					
Spark and recall:	**Introduce:**	**Attempt:**	**Compare:**	**Collaborate:**	**Create:**
Assessment ideas:					

A completed template for a lesson on story openings in a gothic writing unit might look like this:

What do I want students to do? Driving question:					
How do I set the focus for my writing at the start to engage my reader in my gothic story?					
Spark and recall: Look at images to do with gothic writing and categorise them.	**Introduce:** Each image comes from the start of a gothic piece – we are going to look at setting the scene today.	**Attempt:** Have a go at writing your opening in 5 minutes, using the image to support your ideas.	**Compare:** Let's look at this model opening from *The Woman in Black* – how does it compare to your draft? Let's define success criteria.	**Collaborate:** Okay, let's write together, focusing on our success criteria.	**Create:** Now have a go at developing your own piece using a new image. As you write, reflect on what made the model a success.
Assessment ideas: Dialogic discussion	Swap books with partner – ask a question	Circulation; questioning	Questioning	Peer assessment	

Big questions and focused questions

You need to plan your work sequentially, building on the learning that students have already mastered. You can achieve this by threading 'big questions' and 'focused questions' throughout your planning. Big questions are those that translate the main aims of the course or curriculum based on the overarching learning objectives. Focused questions break the big questions down into skills that can be explored in discrete lessons. For example:

- Big question: How is structure used in non-fiction to engage the reader?
- Focused question: What is the impact of using the first person in non-fiction on the reader?

Plotting the big question will likely be the job of your head of department – but it may be your responsibility one day!

Task

Look at the curriculum maps for your subject. What are the overarching aims? What are the high-level goals? Practise turning these into big questions.

Once you have your big questions, you can assess what knowledge, skills and adventure are needed to allow students to answer the question robustly. You can categorise this into what needs revisiting and what will be new concepts for students. For example:

How is structure used in non-fiction to engage the reader?	
Revisit	**New concepts**
What is non-fiction?	Structural features
Reading skills	Exploring alternate viewpoints
Effect on the reader	
Structuring responses with evidence	

From these building blocks, you can extract some focused questions to support your short-term planning. For example:

- How do I identify the effect on the reader?
- How can I structure my response with evidence?
- What are structural features?
- What is a non-fiction piece?

Work out these questions as part of your lesson planning. You can then use them as learning objectives, breaking them down even further within the lesson, scaffolding through questioning.

What are structural features?	
Step	**Planned questioning**
Spark and recall	What interests you about the sentences?
	Which sentence is in the first person? Which is in the third person?
Introduce	What do we mean by 'structure'?
	Which of these might be structural features?
Attempt	How will you use some of these features to engage your reader?
	What do you think is the effect of your piece?
Compare	What structural features can you see in the model?
	How do they impact you as a reader?
	Could you use these in your own piece?
Collaborate	How will we start to structure our piece to engage the reader?
	Is that a language or a structural feature?
	How can we summarise effect?
Create	Which structural features will you use in your piece?
	How do you want your reader to respond?

Reflection

- Could you turn your learning objectives into focused questions?
- Does this help with your assessment of learning?
- Could you use the sequence 'spark and recall' to 'create' in your lessons this week?

A Level

It may be a couple of years before you start teaching at A Level, but it's useful to start thinking early on about how to encourage GCSE students to continue their study of English at higher levels. Considering the value of English skills is a good place to start.

Reading	Writing	Oracy
Understanding of diverse cultures and viewpoints	Crafting arguments	Communication
Analytical thinking	Using evidence to support a stance	Empathy
Research skills	Attention to detail	Problem solving
Critical thinking		Inclusive leadership
		Public speaking
		Confidence and self esteem

There is also the fact that storytelling has huge impact. It is ingrained in all cultures and is a fundamental part of human communication, entertainment and education. Stories have an emotional impact: they can evoke joy, sadness, fear or empathy. The power of feeling a connection and responding authentically to characters and experiences in stories stems from their relatability. This is why stories have become a means of translating values to one another – and an excellent educational tool. They allow us to simplify complex concepts and make them more accessible and memorable. We can use them to persuade others of our point of view, appealing to emotions and logic. Stories inspire and motivate, supporting us in achieving our desired goals. Seeing life through the eyes of diverse characters can help us empathise with people from all walks of life. In this sense, stories can bridge cultural gaps.

Studying English at A Level opens all of these doors for students, making them more empathetic, insightful and understanding. English also complements other subjects with the foundational skills of communication and developed thinking. There is no harm in reminding students of these benefits – and of constantly keeping them in mind yourself!

Key strategies and takeaways

- **English is unique:** Welcome to the profession – English is a joy to teach!
- **Pedagogical schema support oracy, reading and writing:** Using the sequence in the schemas in conjunction with each other can support you as an English teacher.
- **Some cognitive science works in English:** Cognitive load theory, interleaving, elaboration, spaced practice and retrieval practice can all support quality teaching in English.
- **Plan carefully – and plan backwards:** Start with what you want students to achieve, and structure your planning with the right questions.
- **Keep them to A level:** English is a transformative subject: students should relish the opportunity to continue their study.

Chapter 2: The principles of English

Within the schema we explore in Chapters 3, 4 and 5 are interrelated principles that underpin effective English pedagogy. This chapter explores these principles in detail and shows how you can apply them in your classroom to underpin effective teaching.

The key principles are:

- Collaborative experiences (construction, oracy and reading)
- Scaffolds, the gradual release of responsibility and modelling
- Assessment and formative feedback
- Targeted practice with mental models
- Authentic responses and constructions
- Thinking critically
- Questioning.

> **Reflection**
>
> - From an initial read of the principles, rank the principles of English in order of importance.
>
> - Is there anything missing that you think is important to your teaching practice?

Collaborative experiences (construction, oracy and reading)

One of the great joys of English is the opportunity it offers to work together to create something. The most obvious point at which this can be done is in the 'Draft' and 'Compare' sections of the writing schema (see Chapter 5), but there are many other opportunities to work collaboratively in English lessons. Whenever you are presenting new information, give students time to talk together and come up with ideas in response to the information. It may help to structure these discussions with planned questions and/or talking frames. The example that follows shows a combination of the two to structure a think-pair-share activity on *The Iliad*.

Think	Pair	Share
It could be argued that the most important theme in *The Iliad* is revenge, as this is what drives the plot from start to finish. Other themes are war, morality, fate, honour. Where do you see the themes play out? Which do you think the most important?	The theme of X is important because... However, we could argue that X is more prominent due to... I disagree, as I think that...	Which themes can you give me some examples of? Which theme is most important to the events of the epic poem?

You can develop the practice of thinking together in group discussions. To add structure and impact to group work, assign roles to support the discussion of ideas and help students to reach a final consensus. Giving students pointers for what they need to achieve in role really helps them to stay focused and to work collaboratively. It is also productive to ask one student to reflect on the success criteria and to report back to you on good behaviours within the group. This encourages students to metacognitively appraise their efforts.

Figure 2.1 is an example of this, developing a debate from the think-pair-share activity above using Palincsar and Brown's (1984) **reciprocal reading strategies**.

Role: Predictor • Lead the task. • Decide what counter-arguments there may be to motion.	Motion: *This house believes that fate is the most important theme in* The Iliad. Collectively create a speech as proposition or opposition.	**Role: Clarifier** • Ensure all meanings are understood.
Role: Questioner • Generate questions to probe and develop your team's argument.	• Use clear examples from the text. • Make reference to the impact on the reader.	**Role: Summariser** • Summarise all discussions in writing. • Check success criteria and report back to the teacher with good behaviours.

Figure 2.1: Reciprocal reading roles (adapted from Palincsar and Brown, 1984)

Here, students are creating their speech collaboratively, each with a different role in their group. It is also useful to have collaborative construction between the teacher and the students in your writing-focused lessons, with you leading from the front. For example, you could use the following script to set up the collaborative writing task in class.

Okay, we're going to explore how to produce a speech arguing for the motion. We'll start by addressing our audience. Does anyone know how we might do that?

(Possible responses: *Ladies and gentlemen. Members of the opposition. Judges. Good afternoon.*)

Nice. Now we need to make it clear that we are arguing for the proposition.

(Possible response: *I am here to argue that fate is the most important theme in Homer's epic.*)

Okay, that's not bad but I think we could add some vocabulary to emphasise the point.

(Possible response: *I am here to propose that fate is undeniably the most crucial theme in Homer's epic.*)

Better. Let's start with a clear example from the text. Can anyone think of a good one?

(Possible response: *One of the most prominent examples is the prophecy surrounding Achilles. Achilles's fate was sealed when his mother, Thetis, learned that he had two possible destinies: to live a long, peaceful life or to achieve immortal glory in battle but die young.*)

Great, I like the use of a colon here to add extra detail. Does anyone know how Thetis sealed her son's fate?

As you can see, this kind of questioning helps students to develop a response. They will add more detail and improve their phrasing as you prompt them to practise the response aloud and reflect on the success criteria.

The best collaborative work needs explicit ground rules. Chapter 3 explores in more detail how to make these clear and how to ensure that all students follow the guidelines for working together.

Scaffolds, the gradual release of responsibility and modelling

Scaffolding is designed to support cognitive load, introducing new concepts without overwhelming your students. It refers to any kind of support mechanism that you put in place for students. They can gradually build their skills with the support of a scaffold until, eventually, they will have internalised the guidelines and are able to build without support. You don't want your students to have an external scaffold forever; they need to reach a stage where they can achieve success without it – whether that's in English lessons or in the wider world.

An example process for moving from external scaffolds to internalised independence through self-scaffolding would be:

Teacher scaffolds $\rightarrow$ feedback $\rightarrow$ modelling $\rightarrow$ prompting $\rightarrow$ self-scaffolding

You can help students to move through this process by means of correction and talk scaffolds (see below). Feedback is key, as it's important to engage students in how they have achieved success, allowing them to internalise the questions that feedback might generate. The modelling stage clarifies for students what success in a particular task looks like. You should then move on to further scaffolding through the use of prompts. At the final, self-scaffolding stage, students should independently ask themselves questions to support the completion of a task.

Talk scaffolds

Teaching assistants can be helpful talk scaffolds for students. Other talk scaffolds you can use in the classroom include:
- whole-class discussions
- group work (pairs or larger groups)
- drama techniques
- metacognitive modelling.

For example, you could use the drama technique of a 'conscience alley' as a talk scaffold to explore a play you are studying. In this activity, the class forms an 'alley' of two lines. One student, in the role of a character from the play, walks down the middle of the alley while the students on either side call out comments to them about this character's behaviour and actions from two different perspectives. At the end, the 'character' student reflects on these behavioural observations and how the activity made them feel. The students forming the alley should think about how to summarise their view of the character at the play's end, to see how the two opposing views compare to the behavioural observations the 'character' student felt.

Here is an example of how a conscience alley talk task might be structured for *An Inspector Calls*, with the character of Mr Birling walking down the alley:

Students with socialist views	Mr Birling at the play's end	Students supporting Birling
You could have saved her. *Society should look after individuals.* *Losing her job was the start of her demise.*	Teacher questions at the end of the 'alley': • How did you feel? • What might be Birling's emotional state by the end of the play?	*She is only one girl.* *It was her own fault.* *She could stayed in her next job.*

Figure 2.2: An example of a 'conscience alley' activity for Mr Birling in *An Inspector Calls*

Task

Imagine you are teaching the idea of loss through Thomas Hardy's poem 'The Voice'. Create a task that uses talk scaffolds to help students understand the poem.

The Voice

Woman much missed, how you call to me, call to me,
Saying that now you are not as you were
When you had changed from the one who was all to me,
But as at first, when our day was fair.

Can it be you that I hear? Let me view you, then,
Standing as when I drew near to the town
Where you would wait for me: yes, as I knew you then,
Even to the original air-blue gown!

Or is it only the breeze, in its listlessness
Travelling across the wet mead to me here,
You being ever dissolved to wan wistlessness,
Heard no more again far or near?

Thus I; faltering forward,
Leaves around me falling,
Wind oozing thin through the thorn from norward,
And the woman calling.

Visual scaffolds

Visual scaffolds are information or examples presented in a visual format to help students conceptualise the ideas. Charts, diagrams and tables to organise ideas are all useful visual scaffolds in English teaching.

Imagine students are about to tackle a gothic writing task. After an initial 'ideas' phase, students may find a scaffold like the one below useful for planning their writing.

Scene (describe the setting) → shift focus (bring in a character/another focus) → zoom in (focus on one detail) → zoom out (shift focus again)	
Language features	**Structural features**
• Precise description of setting • Emotive language • Atmospheric descriptions • Language that develops • Symbolism ambiguity	• Variety of sentence types to alter pace • Foreshadowing • Third person voice • Shifts in focus • Repetition

Scaffold through prompts

An important technique in analytical writing in English is the use of judicious evidence to support the points being made. Prompting students to develop ideas and evidence is key to securing the skills they need for this. For example, if a student gives an answer that shows some knowledge of a text, you might prompt them to explore *how* they know this. Other useful simple prompts include 'Tell me more' and 'Can you elaborate on that?'.

When planning prompts, it's useful to think about a hierarchy of skills in English. The following table gives some examples.

Reading skills	Prompts	Writing skills	Prompts
Perceptive inferences	Could you delve deeper here?	Convincing and compelling communication	Does the language make you want to read on?
Analysis of language/ structural choices	What language feature gives that effect?	Tone, style and register match audience and purpose	Is the language appropriate for the text type and audience?
Judicious references	How does the structure impact you?	Ambitious vocabulary	Can we vary our language here?
Exploration of differences in texts	How does this differ from X?	Well-crafted language	Could we have more impact with structure?
Sophisticated use of subject terminology	Could you use some terminology here?	Inventive use of structure	
		Linked paragraphs	

Modelling

Eggen and Kauchak (2001) define modelling as an 'instructional activity' in which 'students learn by observing'. Teacher modelling is essential in oracy, reading and writing. It is most effective when you follow the process of teacher modelling → collaborative draft → student construction, so students are actively involved.

First, come up with a model paragraph of the type of writing students should produce, then work as a class to create a collaborative draft, prompting students by referencing success criteria: How might we describe the setting? Could we add some imagery here? What adjectives might add to the effect here? Finally, get students to construct their writing independently using the model as a benchmark of success and giving them some useful vocabulary they can use.

You might use this in the following way to help students create an engaging opening for a piece of gothic writing.

Teacher model	Collaborative draft	Student construction
The moon hung low in the ink-black sky, casting long shadows across the desolate landscape. The wind howled through the gnarled branches of the ancient oak trees, their leaves rustling like whispers of the damned.	*The sky was...* *The ancient rowan swayed...* *A thick, impenetrable mist crawled...*	Useful vocabulary: • impenetrable • desolate • damned

Task

For the gothic opening above, decide what success criteria you would give students to support them with their draft.

Metacognitive modelling

As you model an example response, speak aloud your thought process so that students can understand how you create the model and can replicate the process in their own writing. You need to:
- narrate your own thinking
- ask questions about what you are producing
- change your writing based on these questions.

This table shows a model paragraph of persuasive speech and the kind of thought tracking you could share with students.

| I am arguing that social media is bad for society. Social media has changed how we interact with one another, sometimes for good, but I must look at the negative consequences of this transformation in communication. | • I need to talk directly to my audience – what techniques can I include to do this? *I'll use personal pronouns like 'you' and 'us'*

 • My stance on the motion needs to be clear. *I'll clarify my language here using 'injurious impact' to make clear my negative stance.*

 • I want to engage my audience. How can I use vocabulary to do this? *I'll chose words like 'revolutionised' and 'transformation' to convey the extent of the change.* | Today, I stand before you to address a growing concern that affects us all, whether we acknowledge it or not: the injurious impact of social media on human communication. We live in an era where technology and social media platforms have revolutionised the way we interact, but it's essential to critically examine the consequences of this digital transformation. |

You can also metacognitively model reading using the reciprocal reading strategies we looked at in Figure 2.1: predict, clarify, question and summarise.

Predict	Clarify
If there are clouds in the sky, what time of year might it be?	What does 'cirrus' mean?
They are purple and orange – what time of day does this suggest?	What might 'heralding' mean?
	When is twilight?
	What might 'pay homage' mean?
Wisps of cirrus clouds painted in shades of coral and lavender began to streak across the heavens, heralding the twilight's arrival. The air, previously buzzing with the energy of the day, grew still, as if nature itself paused to pay homage to the impending masterpiece.	
Question	**Summarise**
What might the 'impending masterpiece' be?	Twilight has beautiful colours after a busy day and the upcoming sunset will be stunning.
What is the impact of using the description 'the heavens'?	
What does 'buzzing' suggest?	

Figure 2.3: Modelling reading using reciprocal reading strategies

You can go through each stage of reciprocal reading in isolation, using pre-planned questioning to support your modelling of a close reading of a text. As you use these different scaffolds and model for students, you will gradually be releasing responsibility to them.

You can follow the sequence of teacher instruction through careful modelling, chunking information to manage cognitive load.

- Question students to assess understanding of the success criteria for the model response.
- Then move into collaborative construction, where you give some responsibility to the students but continue to guide them in production.
- The student then attempts the task, working towards the focused question for the lesson. Here you can continue to guide with scaffolds and questioning.
- Finally, students complete the task separately, developing authenticity.

Compare	Collaborate	Attempt	Create
Scaffold		$\longrightarrow$	Independence
Modelling by the teacher Chunking information	Collaborative constructions Metacognitive modelling	Scaffold for speaking/ writing	Freedom Creativity
Questioning			

Figure 2.4: Gradual release of responsibility (adapted from Spires and Stone, 1989)

This gradual release of responsibility can happen in one lesson or over a series of lessons as you work your way to a summative task.

Assessment and formative feedback

Peer- and self-assessment

As you have seen, encouraging students to actively engage with feedback is essential to their development in English. They need to be able to think metacognitively in order to apply successful thought processes to future tasks. To help students understand what success in a task looks like, it is important to model good examples and outcomes for them, and then scaffold assessment with success criteria so that students can first self-assess their own responses, and then peer assess their classmates' work effectively.

When modelling, make sure students understand that there will be equally successful variations on the model – there is never only one definitive answer or 'right' way of structuring a response, especially in creative writing. In this regard, it helps to focus on what the reader should feel or experience rather than hard-and-fast rules about how to get there. For example, if you were modelling analytical paragraphs, you would not necessarily want students to mimic the exact structure of the model; to help them steer clear of this, focus on what the reader should experience when digesting analytical writing.

Model: How is fate explored in *Romeo and Juliet*?	What the reader should experience	Look for...
Fate is a central and recurring theme in the play. The play opens with a prologue that explicitly states that the love between Romeo and Juliet is 'star-crossed', suggesting that their destinies are predetermined by the stars. This connotes the idea of it being out of human control and inevitable. This immediately introduces to the audience the idea of fate playing a crucial role in the unfolding tragedy.	• An understanding that fate is a key theme. • Evidence from the play to support this assertion. • Time to explore some connotations with that evidence. • Time to reflect on the impact on the audience.	• References to fate. • Judicious evidence from the play. • Connotations with the evidence. • Exploration of the impact on the audience.

Marshall and Wiliam (2006) state that learning intentions and success criteria should always be shared with students. It is not always easy to translate to students what constitutes a 'good' response in English, but one way of sharing success criteria is by modelling good practice. It is also useful to sequence activities in lessons in such a way that students' understanding of quality develops. Allow students time to think for themselves about any criteria for improvement so that they are actively involved in their own learning and knowledge creation.

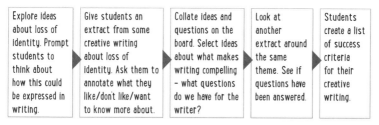

Explore ideas about loss of identity. Prompt students to think about how this could be expressed in writing. ▶ Give students an extract from some creative writing about loss of identity. Ask them to annotate what they like/don't like/want to know more about. ▶ Collate ideas and questions on the board. Select ideas about what makes writing compelling – what questions do we have for the writer? ▶ Look at another extract around the same theme. See if questions have been answered. ▶ Students create a list of success criteria for their creative writing.

Figure 2.5: An example sequence to develop understanding of success criteria and encourage metacognition

In this example, students are actively involved in critiquing two models. This allows them to experience the text as a reader and prepares them to become writers; it also provides robust success criteria through the questioning of the texts, to prepare them for peer and self-assessment.

Formative feedback

To keep students on a trajectory of improvement, try to foster a culture of feedback in your classroom. As you plan, you need to know where your students are, where they're going and how you can get them there. Your students need to know this too – especially where they're going and how to get there!

There are several more specific reasons why feedback is important:

- It clarifies misconceptions. For example, students might think that *Macbeth* is an Elizabethan play rather than a Jacobean one, or they may think that Jekyll and Hyde are different characters. Feedback can identify these misconceptions and give you the opportunity to revisit and clarify ideas.
- It increases motivation and boosts confidence. Knowing what they're doing well supports students, and understanding how to improve motivates them, as does reflecting on their improvements once they have started responding to improvement goals.
- It encourages metacognitive learning and self-regulation. Knowing what success looks like and reflecting on their own work and how effective it is supports students through the learning process. The more they understand their own processes and strategies, the more successful learning development will be.
- It develops communication skills. Feedback demands understanding and the implementation of various actions. It helps students to express themselves clearly across contexts.
- It develops critical-thinking skills. Developing a metacognitive mindset in the process of receiving feedback forces students to think critically about their work. They need to assess their levels of success and consider alternative approaches.
- It enhances the culture of your classroom. A culture of positive feedback will help students realise that it's okay to feel vulnerable and to accept support from each other. Just as you feed back constructively as a teacher, you can support students in feeding back effectively to their peers.

Feedback needs to be integrated into your planning. It can be designed as short, verbal responses or more detailed written comments. Use this simple feedback loop to ensure you keep revisiting and adjusting ideas through feedback:

Question $\rightarrow$ identify misconceptions or errors $\rightarrow$ adapt teaching

To ensure that students can also engage in peer assessment, it's vital to make the expectations for feedback transparent. Feedback should be:

- open – individuals should feel comfortable sharing their thoughts
- constructive and based on success criteria – focus on the curriculum to help students develop and improve
- regular and timely – provided on a regular basis and soon after work has been produced
- reciprocal – teachers should take feedback from students
- goal-orientated – links to specific objectives or focused questions for the lesson/big questions for the term should be made.

The following table outlines some techniques you could use to embed quality **formative assessment** in your classroom.

Exit tickets	Ask students the big question for the lesson as they leave: 'How is Romeo presented in this scene? Use a subordinate clause to add impact to your idea.'
Metacognition matrix	Get students to pick two or three sentence starters from a matrix to conclude: 'Three things I have learned today are . . .', 'A question I have about today's lesson is . . .'.
Spot the misconception	Give students a piece of work with a misconception (some writing out of genre; an analysis with an inappropriate interpretation) and see, through dialogic teaching, if they can spot it.
Self-assessment	Give students clear success criteria and ask them to self-assess their final piece of work.
Formative assessment grids	These can be used in writing or speaking where you can give a mark out of 5 for things like structure, response to arguments, originality, word use.
Low-stakes quiz	At the end or at the mid-way point of the lesson, have quizzes where it's okay for students to make mistakes and improve.

Embedding formative assessment in each lesson will ensure you are pitching correctly. It will also allow students to see that formative rather than summative judgements can have power. When students read their own pieces, encourage them to have a formative response to the writing and to realise the processes that lead to crafted writing. I would encourage you to have a culture of sharing and discussing work in class – both models and students' own responses. Hearing students share work is beneficial to you as a teacher and can give you the opportunity to formatively intervene. It's also really beneficial for learners to hear other's work and to see what success can look like. This works well with both creative and analytical writing.

Precise praise improves feedback

Marshall and Wiliam (2006) explain that the manner in which feedback is delivered can affect how it is received and, consequently, the impact it has. Be really focused on the objectives of the task in your feedback, giving precise praise and being very clear about what the student has done well.

Having specific success criteria in mind when planning your lesson will really help with this. For example, imagine you were teaching dialogically through debate with a lesson built around the question: *Is censorship of art and media ever justified?* You might plan your questions and precise praise as follows:

How can I use persuasive features to engage my audience?		
Success criteria: Understanding of what makes a piece persuasive; clear opinions on the motion, backed up with evidence; explorations of impact on stakeholders; selection of effective structural and linguistic rhetorical devices.		
	Planned questioning	**Potential precise praise**
Spark and recall	Which sentence is more persuasive? Why?	You have supported your idea with clear reasoning.
Introduce	What is your opinion on the motion? Why do you think this?	You have been clear about your opinion and supported this with evidence.
Attempt	Discuss with your partner: How does the evidence support or discredit the motion? Who are the stakeholders here? How are they impacted?	You have been discerning in selecting stakeholders and clear about the impact.
Compare	Let's hear a model speech. What did you like/dislike? What structural features had impact? What language features were persuasive?	You have selected a feature and explored its effect.
Collaborate	In your groups, construct a response to the motion using the features which engage and persuade. How can the scaffolds on the board help you?	You have used the scaffold to undermine the opposition effectively.
Create	Which persuasive features will you use in your speech? How do you want your audience to respond?	You have selected a persuasive structural feature.

Verbal feedback can be powerful, but of course you may also need to provide written feedback on a task. To make this effective try to build in time for responses to feedback in your planning. A good way to ensure student responses is to ask further questions. For example, imagine students have now written the speech they were working on in the lesson above. Here is an example of a student statement and questions you could ask in writing to encourage a response:

Censorship of art is integral to protecting our communities from harm. Dangerous ideologies may be communicated through art.

There is clear reasoning here for your opinion. What might the impact of this be on society? Is freedom of expression a human right? Could you explore this further?

To support you when it comes to marking, try selecting the key skills you want students to develop at each level of writing and creating a code for these, linked to appropriate feedback/questions, ahead of time. A graduated code for a persuasive piece might be:

A	Can you make it clear which side of the motion you are on, using a *because* statement in your next paragraph?
B	What evidence is there for what you state? Embed some clear evidence into your next paragraph.
C	What is the impact of your argument on society? Explore the impact on stakeholders in your next paragraph.
D	Is there a counter-argument to what you say? Explore and undermine it in your next paragraph.
E	Could you develop your language here to engage further? Embed the phrases 'prevailing beliefs' and 'stifling creativity' in your next paragraph.

This will allow you to give students some precise praise and a letter to refer to when completing their response, which will save you time, as well as keeping feedback structured and useful. You can circulate as students complete their improved paragraphs and ask them to highlight where they have added material in response to the feedback.

Another important aspect of assessment and feedback is identifying trends across the class – common misconceptions and similar responses from students. You can then craft model responses that eradicate these misconceptions or demonstrate the skills you would like students to develop. As an example of this, I had a class that was not responding to the opposition in the debate task above, based on the question *Is censorship of art and media ever justified?* There was little undermining of the counterarguments.

I decided to show them the following model before they responded to feedback on the motion:

> *You may say that censorship will only have limited effectiveness. Indeed, it is true that banned content can still circulate through underground channels, making censorship measures less impactful. We cannot justify not censoring content just because of this. We have a responsibility to protect public morality. Censorship can protect the public from exposure to explicit content that may be considered morally offensive or harmful, particularly to children and vulnerable individuals. It is clear that censoring this will ensure that most content is protected, ensuring that children are safe to enjoy and learn from art.*

I then dialogically explored the impact of having a counterargument that was overrun by a powerful argument in favour of the stance. This helped prepare students to respond to my marking.

You can support students in self- and peer-assessment by encouraging them to ask questions of one another in line with success criteria. For example, you might be exploring the impact of language in an extract from *A Christmas Carol* and have asked students to peer-assess their partner's analytical paragraph. It would be useful to give students an idea of the questions they could ask, using the following visual scaffold.

Success criteria		Question
Judicious evidence	A	Could you use some evidence from the text to support your point?
Connotations with language	B	Could you zoom in on evidence and explore the connotations of key words?
	C	What is the impact of the language on the Victorian reader?
Exploration of Dickens' purpose	D	What is Dickens's message here? Could you explore it?
Some contextual exploration	E	How might a modern reader respond to this?
		Create your own question in line with the success criteria!

Reflection

- Reflect on your lessons this week – have you embedded models to ensure students know what success looks like?
- Can you articulate what the reader should feel from a piece so that you can translate this to success criteria?
- How can you instil the right culture for feedback in your classroom?

Targeted practice with mental models

Students need to create mental models of success in order to internalise scaffolds. Getting students to practise explaining a concept to each other in pairs can help them to develop mental models. For example, they could try explaining how to structure a piece of non-fiction writing, or how a tenor, vehicle and ground makes a metaphor. You can also ask questions to help students link different pieces of knowledge: Why might Scrooge behave this way? Why is Juliet's father so angry? After that, students need to apply knowledge to complete an independent task, such as completing an analytical paragraph in response to the question 'How do patriarchal standards affect Juliet in the play?'

Some examples of **mental models** and activities that will help students to access them are outlined in the following table.

Mental model	Description	Activities
Vocabulary web	Students build mental networks of words – antonyms and synonyms.	Word blast (Chapter 4)
Reading analysis	Students explain strategies for understanding and interpreting texts.	Reciprocal reading (Chapter 4) Reading schema
Writing process	Students use mental models for the writing process (prewriting, drafting, editing).	Writing scaffolds (Chapter 5) Free writing
Group-work process	Students have mental models for effective communication based on ground rules (see Chapter 3).	Debates Reciprocal reading group roles

If students find it difficult to make connections, it may help to isolate a specific part of the mental model and develop it through targeted practice. For example, students might struggle to use complex sentences at the drafting stage of their writing; in this case you could use the following series of activities to embed understanding of the issue and clarify how the mental model would work.

Teacher	Collaboration	Student
Model how to change a series of simple sentences into a complex sentences for added detail and engagement. *You never really understand a person until you consider things from his point of view, until you climb into his skin and walk around in it.* (*To Kill a Mockingbird* by Harper Lee)	Let's work together to write something about empathy. *We need to feel. . .* What might be a poignant end to this sentence? How can we ensure it is complex and engaging? Let's repeat 'feel': *. . ., feel keenly so that we. . .*	Describe the feeling of empathy using complex sentences. Some sentence starters you might use would be: *To understand we need to. . ., then we need to. . .* *Empathy means. . ., therefore we must decide to. . .*

Authentic responses and constructions

Although Ofsted's Research Review for English does not mention creativity (Ofsted, 2022), Cremin and Myhill (2012) identify language as a creative, dialogic medium, and creativity is obviously an essential part of the subject. We can be creative in English in two distinct ways:

- by exploring the impact that language has on us
- by using language to create meaning.

Students are often asked to create something at the end of a lesson or teaching series, but you can also elicit creative responses from them throughout lessons. Creativity starts with innovation – coming up with something new. That might be having a unique perspective on a piece of text or an original way of expressing ideas. Breaking away from scaffolds and constraints, encourage your students to be as innovative as possible. In tandem with this, students should be creating something meaningful, writing with emotional resonance and reading from a critical and insightful viewpoint. Creativity includes divergent thinking – exploring alternative points of view or synthesising knowledge from different sources to create something new.

Imagination is the foundation of authentic creativity – not to mention an essential part of having fun. Encouraging your students to visualise ideas and explore possibilities for their writing will secure their love of the subject. Enhance this through a varied expression of creative ideas, including art, writing and performance and make sure students feel comfortable taking an adaptable approach to their work. Flexibility will support students' creativity.

Some students may respond quickly to the opportunity to be creative, but others may be more reticent. Practice and exposure to new experiences in the classroom will help all students to develop their creative instincts, and for that you will need good stimuli in the form of a diverse range of texts and ideas.

In 1866, George Eliot commented that 'aesthetic teaching is the highest of all teaching because it deals with life in its highest complexity'. This idea – that inspirational, creative teaching is the most valuable – plays into the point I made earlier about the importance of the *adventure* of English and the principles of authenticity. You need to encourage authentic responses and constructions in your classroom by allowing students to form their own ideas and follow their own paths. When you read something new with your students, ask them what they like, what they dislike, what speaks to them. Get them personally involved in the response to the text.

Chapter 5 explores in detail how to encourage students to write authentically, but at a basic level allowing students time to respond to a stimulus 'cold' is good practice for getting them comfortable with their own voice in writing. Try this free writing with your students: give them a short stimulus, such as an image or the first line of their piece, and ask them just to write whatever comes into their head. Make sure they know that no one will read this writing – it's just a practice exercise to get their creativity flowing.

Diversity in the curriculum

In English, we are lucky to be able to teach through the medium of stories. Storytelling is an excellent pedagogical approach and humans have always used stories to pass on wisdom and spur imagination. Students should be able to relate to the stories they read, and the characters and ideas contained within them. As such, it's key to include a variety of texts in your classroom examples and to make sure you include writers that might be underrepresented in set texts and typical example extracts.

It's useful to assess the representation of protected characteristics in the curriculum: age, disability, gender reassignment, marriage and civil partnership, pregnancy and maternity, 'race', religion or belief, sex, and sexual orientation. Most of the research you will find on diversification has been through the lens of 'race' or ethnicity. This is important, and there are many useful resources that will help you to introduce a diverse range of texts in your lessons.

Thinking critically

The next principle to play a key part in any English classroom is critical thinking. Willingham (2019) states that to be critical, thinking has to be novel, self-directed and effective.

Characteristic	Explanation	Example
Novel	We are not just drawing on memory, we are applying what we know to a new situation.	Identifying a caesura and its impact in an unseen poem.
Self-directed	We are not just following instructions from someone else; we are involved in the thinking itself.	Evaluating a text through our own guided questioning.
Effective	We are considering both sides of an argument, ensuring that ideas are supported with evidence and using logic to reason.	Exploring critical readings of a text.

Critical thinking is authentic, self-guided and well-practised, so background knowledge is one of its main building blocks. Using existing knowledge and encouraging students to make connections will help them to build their background knowledge, which will prove invaluable when interrogating a text and exploring its impact creatively.

The following is an example of a sequence that could be developed for poetry.

Poem	Voice	Language	Structure	Ambiguity	Response
What is the subject? What words stand out?	Who is speaking? What might they be trying to say? How are they feeling?	What language is used? What is its impact?	How is the poem structured? How does this affect the reader?	Is there any ambiguous meaning?	How do you as the reader respond? What other responses might there be?

Repeating this process in different contexts will crystalise it in your students' minds. Willingham explains how knowledge like this impacts thinking in three ways:

1. Recognising multiple simpler solutions from memory can support complex critical thinking (for example, exploring the ambiguous response to an unseen poem can be supported with knowledge of what an extended metaphor is).
2. Recognition of knowledge helps students to analyse and evaluate more quickly.
3. Experience allows students to group elements of thinking to save space in the working memory (for example, caesura, enjambment and internal rhyme work together to create one structural effect).

Bringing all these factors into play will enable your students to express a novel response to a text, to use a mental model to self-direct themselves through a critical analysis, and to think effectively.

Elaborative questions can also play a part in developing critical thinking. Extending student thinking with a 'response to the response' question is really useful in encouraging higher-order thinking. Below is an example of how this might work in a discussion of themes in *A Christmas Carol*.

Student responses	Response to the response
Generosity and compassion are key themes in the novel.	Could you give me some examples of that?
	Could you elaborate more on your point?
	How might a Victorian reader view this?
As the story is about a miserly man, I feel greed is the key theme.	Interesting... does this theme centre on any specific character?
I think time is a significant theme.	What was Dickens' intent here?
	How do you respond to this?

You can also hone critical thinking by enhancing **reasoning** – specifically, inductive reasoning – through discussion. The conclusions reached through inductive reasoning aren't necessarily true, but they are probabilistic. An example of inductive reasoning based on *Sense and Sensibility* might be:
- Men in Georgian England would visit women they felt affection for or intended to marry.
- Edward has promised to visit Elinor.
- Edward feels affection for Elinor.

You can encourage reasoning through structured discussion, making sure that students' thinking is effective by establishing success criteria. For example, you could set the following task and success criteria:

Task: How does Edward feel about Elinor?

In your groups:
- *Decide on a conclusive idea by considering both sides of the argument.*
- *Use evidence to support your responses.*
- *Reflect on the behaviour of men at the time and how this aligns with Edward's actions.*

It is worth deciding what inductive reasoning you would like students to make, in order to prompt them in such a way that they can reason logically. What background knowledge do they need to draw on to reach critical conclusions, for example? Draw this out of their thinking. You could use a mental model for character when reading texts with students. For example:

My character is...	My objective is...	My tactics are...	Evidence for this is...	Context that impacts me includes...
Who am I?	What do I want?	How do I behave to get what I want?	Where is this seen in the story?	What social, historical or cultural context impacts me?

Reflection

- What tasks could you embed in your lessons to develop creativity?
- How can you ensure thinking is novel, self directed and effective?
- What is in your sphere of influence to change about diversity in your classroom?

Questioning

The most powerful thing you can do to encourage thought in the classroom is to ask questions. Memory is a residue of thought (Willingham, 2009), so if you want students to store knowledge and skills in their long-term memory, you need to get them thinking by asking the right questions. Rosen's (2017) question matrix is a fabulous tool for trainee teachers, categorising questions into 24 prompts that Rosen believes define the way that students talk. Of the 24, the six most important (in my opinion) are as follows:

Type	Description	Example
Authentic	Where we relate the information to us.	Have you ever...?
Text-based	Where we relate one part of the text to another or to another text.	Does this remind you of...?
Word-based	Where we make comments about meaning.	Where does the text say...?
Probing	Where we explore and are tentative about something.	Is anything missing from...?
Theoretical	Where we speculate what might happen/what could have happened.	What might have...?
Meditative	Where we make interpretations often starting with 'I think'.	What do you think?

Think about this in the sense of questions developing from being about the individual, moving through the text itself, to ideas beyond the text and finally reaching a conclusive meditative stance.

When planning questioning, include wait time. When asking open questions and looking for answers requiring demonstration of higher-order skills, you could wait up to 15 seconds for a response (Mujis and Reynolds, 2011). This will give students the time to formulate a deeper level response.

Reflection
- How would you rank the principles for English now? Have any of them changed position?
- How might you embed questioning into your daily practice?

Key strategies and takeaways

- **Teach knowledge, skills and adventure:** These are the three key elements to English that you can develop using the schemas in the next three chapters of this book.
- **Principles are like a golden thread:** There are several principles for English teaching, explored throughout the book, which you should try to integrate into your planning and practice.
- **Students must be engaged in their learning:** To engage in assessment and understand success, students must be actively involved in learning and in building mental models.
- **Authentic creativity should permeate the classroom:** Making time for authentic responses and ideas is key to the best English teaching.
- **Diversity is crucial:** Including a diverse range of texts in the curriculum will give students a sense of belonging.
- **Encourage critical thinking:** Embed this skill in your classroom.
- **Question your students:** Questions structure planning, and the best lessons make use of pre-planned questions.
- **Model, model, model:** Showing students success and metacognitively thinking them through the process gives them the tools for success.

Chapter 3: Oracy in the classroom

Why talk?

It might seem strange to begin with a chapter on oracy, preceding those on reading and writing, as it has long been the practice in the English classroom to focus on reading first and then think about how to write a response to a text. However, I believe that oracy (the skill of speaking and listening) is the most important element of learning and should be prioritised, because this is how we begin to communicate.

Oracy is a neologism, first used in the 1960s by Professor Andrew Wilkinson of the University of East Anglia, to give the practice the same priority as literacy and numeracy (CUPA, 2022). You learn to listen before you speak, and to speak before you read, so these are critical skills to acquire. Evidence suggests that some disadvantaged students may be behind their more advantaged peers in terms of spoken language when starting school (Education Endowment Foundation, 2021). These gaps can grow as students progress through school, affecting not only their ability to find employment when leaving education, but also their mental health in later life.

Oracy Cambridge and Voice 21 categorise the separate elements of oracy as:
- cognitive elements: what we talk about, how we question things, how we organise our speech, the judgements we make
- the language we use: the vocabulary, register and style we choose
- the physical elements of our speech: how our voice sounds, our pace and tone, and non-verbal features, such as how much eye contact we make
- the social and emotional element of oracy: how we listen to others and respond, our confidence in speaking, our awareness of the audience and how we work with others.

(Oracy Cambridge and Voice 21, 2020)

Thinking about these discrete elements can be very useful when devising success criteria for oracy. You can focus on one element at a time in the preparation for group work or speeches, and your success criteria should give a good idea of what successful communication looks like. It is essential to build development of the sensory parts of speech, to support the cognitive elements, to refine and foster language, and to ensure that students hone their skills of connection so that they interact and collaborate well.

The GCSE English Language exam no longer has a speaking and listening element that contributes to students' final marks, but never forget that you're preparing students for much more than just exams, and there are countless benefits to nurturing oracy in the classroom. To begin with, oracy escalates engagement in learning. Embedding effective spoken communication encourages learners to think critically and to reason confidently, while enhancing their vocabulary and their ability to express themselves accurately in writing as well as speech. It also equips students with the tools to engage in further study, work and democratic life beyond school. Oracy interventions can provide support to struggling students to help them catch up, with frequent interventions over sustained periods proving to be the most successful, according to the EEF (2021). Talk also allows students the opportunity to express their views eloquently and to make sense of their feelings and responses. It is an initiation into the realm of rhetoric.

Listening kindly and critically is also essential outside the classroom. These skills can ignite a social conscience in students and support progress towards social equity – the main reason I became a teacher.

Reflection

- Do you use any talk in your classroom? If so, how well do students respond?
- What are the barriers to using listening and speaking in your lessons?
- How might Oracy Cambridge and Voice 21's oracy framework direct your planning?

Pedagogical schema for oracy

It can be useful to structure oracy instruction through a schema. For example:

Oracy	Engage	Contribute	Explore	Challenge	Concur	Reflect
	Hook students with explicit listening activities.	Set ground rules so that everyone can be involved.	Allow time for students to consider new material and apply reasoning.	Use questioning and cognitive conflict.	Seek agreement.	Use **metacognition** to explore what's been learned.

The following sections explore each element of the schema and make suggestions for how you could scaffold them effectively in your classroom.

Engage: Making listening explicit

It is important to make listening skills explicit to learners, as often these are not discussed or modelled in an obvious way. So, how do we listen? When I worked as a literacy lead, I learned a lot from the approach taken in modern languages, and I adapted their process to work in the English classroom. This is based on promoting five key skills:

1. Make sure that students *understand the goal*: Are your students listening for instructions to a task or are they finding out new information about a character? Make sure they understand the purpose of their listening.
2. Give them time to *reflect*: Once they have heard the new information, allow students time to process it in line with structured questions so they fully understand what has been said.
3. Pause to *summarise*: Get students to paraphrase the new information by summarising it aloud or in their notebooks.
4. Make time to *share*: Collaboratively share what has been learned and support students to make links to other ideas from their working memory.
5. Finally, *clarify*: Check that everyone has understood and selected the key information by redefining the goal.

The following example shows these skills applied to a task involving the poem 'Thirteen' by Caleb Femi in the AQA GCSE poetry anthology *Worlds and Lives*.

Task: As you listen to the poem, decide what 'Thirteen' by Caleb Femi says about institutional racism.

This decision can come through discussion with others, having listened to and read the poem, using the framework on the next page as a structure.

Understand the goal: Understand Femi's purpose and ideas about racism.

Reflect: How is the innocence of primary school contrasted with the way the boy is questioned by the police?

Summarise: What is the effect of the repetition of the word 'thirteen'? Does it suggest the poet's purpose?

Share: Are students aware of any other texts written about the same time (2000) that also question racism?

Clarify: Clarify Femi's purpose and ideas.

The poem highlights the racism of the time as the forces (the police), supposedly there for our protection, demonise a young Black boy.

It is important to keep the listening process active and ensure that it works towards specific success criteria. For example, success criteria for the task above might be:

- Explore the poet's ideas and purpose.
- Explore themes within the text.
- Identify language techniques and explore their effect.
- Make comparisons with different texts/information.

It is useful to outline these success criteria for students before the task itself; you can then reflect on them at the end of the task when clarifying. There is also an opportunity to introduce a metacognitive element here, encouraging students to reflect on how successfully they have completed the task.

Task

Copy the table. Think about a poem you will be teaching and some new information you want your students to listen to and focus on. Note these in the middle column. Then decide on your success criteria: what do you want students to explore? Write these in the left-hand column. Finally, note down your questions for each stage of the listening process on the right.

Success criteria	Poem/information	Key skills questions
		Understand the goal:
		Reflect:
		Summarise:
		Share:
		Clarify:

Below are some suggestions for activities you can use to help structure listening in the classroom.

Listening bingo

This exercise can lead to some fruitful talk. It's based on the 2022 winner of the Grammy for the Best Spoken Word Album, Don Cheadle's narration of *Carry On: Reflections For A New Generation* by US civil rights activist and congressman John Lewis. It's an engaging listen, beautifully read. Cheadle comments that 'humility' could be the title of this book, and its poignant themes will appeal to students in all contexts.

Playing the book's opening passage alongside a listening bingo grid like the one below will support students' comprehension and enable them to make links between the historical context and Lewis's actions. Students should highlight the phrases as they hear them.

Purity of heart	Voted not to participate	Majority in Nashville didn't agree with the sit-ins	I'm marching as John Lewis, a citizen of Alabama
Focused on what was absolutely and spiritually essential	Theologian	Deter	Ego politics

You can then unpick the meaning of each word or phrase through structured questions about the passage, zooming in on terms like 'ego politics' and breaking them down to allow students to predict meanings based on prior knowledge (they may know 'ego', for instance). These questions should ensure that students are not just listening for words out of context, but can also identify where these phrases come in the text and how they direct the meaning of the text. It is useful to plan these questions before you teach, in order to set a clear goal for the exercise, to reflect after the listening, and to summarise.

Example questions include:
- How did John Lewis deal with issues?
- Where is John Lewis from?
- How does he feel about this?
- Why is it necessary for him to say he is a 'citizen'?
- What were the sit-ins?
- Who supported them?
- Did that stop John Lewis?
- Who was playing ego politics? What might this mean?

You could then have a class discussion based on the question 'How does congressman John Lewis reveal his motivations for joining the civil rights movement?' Give credit for students using the vocabulary they have highlighted from the listening exercise, and use structured questions to help them expand their ideas.

You could provide synonyms (for example, *avert*, *block* or *discourage* for 'deter') to help students discuss the themes of the book.

Scaffolded listening

Listening can be scaffolded in much the same way as reading (see Chapter 4). For example, you could use another form of listening bingo to focus on comprehension, using pictures to explore the use of imagery in an extract from Shakespeare.

Imagine your group is listening to extracts from Act II of *A Midsummer Night's Dream*, in which Oberon and Titania have a variety of encounters. The goal of the listening activity is to explore the relationship between the two fairies, with the leading question 'How is the relationship between Oberon and Titania portrayed in Act II?'. Give students a copy of the grid below and ask them to listen out for the quotations on it and also for language that is reflected in the images.

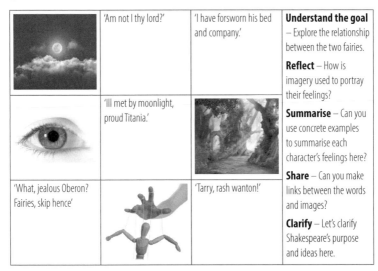

Figure 3.1: A matrix for listening bingo

Students could complete this task in pairs – again with structured questioning to facilitate their discussion – guided by the five key skills: understand the goal, reflect, summarise, share, clarify. For example, students may discuss how they heard some friction between the characters and a desire for control, which they may identify with the puppeteer image in the grid. This could lead to a discussion about who holds the power in the relationship.

Some structured post-listening questions to support comprehension might be:
- What adjectives do the fairies use to describe one another?
- What does this say about them?
- Does Titania want to be close to Oberon?
- What might a green eye suggest?
- Who holds the power here?
- Could the exchange between the fairies be read in any other ways? If so, how?

Contribute: Making sure everyone is involved

To encourage all students to participate, it is important to make your classroom dialogic and exploratory. This will demand interaction through involvement and allow students to articulate their thinking verbally (National Literacy Trust, 2012).

The 'dialogic climate' was conceived by Robin Alexander in the early 2000s. It refers to *continuous* talk, enabling contributors to build and develop ideas. The aim of such talk is to achieve a collective understanding through questioning and discussion. Alexander states that teaching dialogically means setting up an ethos for talk that is collective, reciprocal, supportive, cumulative and purposeful (Alexander, 2020). Key ideas within this approach include:
- asking questions starting with 'How' and 'Why'
- balancing recall with probing questions
- feeding back in the form of more in-depth questions
- using strategies such as 'no hands up' to elicit more responses.

Alexander also believes that this ethos for talk can be further developed if it is taught in a sequence:
- Set a clear goal.
- Deconstruct a model.
- Make talk visible by metacognitively highlighting the successful traits (perhaps using Voice 21's framework).
- Unpick grammatical features.
- Carry out pair rehearsals of a final talk or writing task.
- Provide speaking frames to scaffold the discussion.

Linked to this is the idea of exploratory talk, conceived by Neil Mercer in 2008. In exploratory talk, partners offer constructive criticism of one another's opinions.

Someone may challenge their partner, but they should give reasons and suggest alternatives to their ideas. In this kind of talk the goal is to seek agreement, and reasoning should be evident in any discussion. Mercer also suggests building an ethos for talk, in the form of explicit ground rules. He believes that a teacher's questions should elevate students to higher-order thinking, creating some conflict in thought. Activities should be framed using open-ended questions and students need to summarise their responses formally (in notes) so they can apply metacognition by reflecting on their thought processes. The teacher must model talk for the students by, for example, giving them frames for agreeing or disagreeing – for example, 'This is a perceptive response. However, I believe....'.

We will explore some specific strategies to enhance these talk types later in the chapter, but first let's consider how Alexander's dialogic climate and Mercer's exploratory talk could help us to establish some ground rules to develop the right ethos for talk in the classroom.

Reflection

What ground rules could you put in place to facilitate contribution and a good class discussion? Take a moment to reflect on the following ideas.

- Encourage everyone in the group to contribute.
- Listen carefully to each other.
- Treat each other's ideas and opinions with respect.
- Only one person should speak at a time.
- Ask people to share the reasons for their ideas.
- Aim to reach a consensus.

What, if anything, would you add to this list of rules to ensure that talk is collective, reciprocal, supportive, cumulative and purposeful?

Alexander sets out specific 'talk moves' for dialogic teaching to encourage contribution in the classroom: questioning, extending (or elaborating), discussing and arguing. I would add reasoning and debating to this list. We will consider all of these as we work through the remainder of the steps of the oracy schema in the rest of the chapter.

Explore through talk

The next stage of the schema is to explore the information through high-quality discussion. Talk enables thinking – and we remember what we think about! This kind of talk increases the time available for tasks and improves motivation and engagement, so you can spend longer exploring information with your class. It is also a useful tool to help you identify any misconceptions students may have.

The following table outlines some foundations for facilitating a fruitful exploratory discussion in your classroom.

Example	Method
Model expectations for behaviour.	Identify good talk behaviours (ground rules). Make these explicit.
Set clear objectives (goals for the discussion).	Establish these clearly before the task. Have a summariser who reflects on the objectives at the end of talk.
Use talk trios.	A and B discuss; C summarises.
Scaffold discussions.	Provide students with key arguments and vocabulary, set up Socratic circles (see below).

A **Socratic circle** is a popular means of discussion that works well to enhance the exploratory element that Mercer advocates. Socratic talk, which dates back to ancient Greece, is essentially talk about talk. It involves an outer circle of students observing an inner circle of their peers while they are engaged in discussion. The outer group uses a range of questions provided by the teacher to help them listen to and evaluate the quality of the inner circle's talk, so they can provide feedback at the end of the discussion.

The inner discussion group (usually 4–6 students) should be given a topic to discuss and guidelines for the discussion which, according to the National Literacy Trust (2012), should include:
- a clear purpose
- defined time limits
- a clear audience (the students observing them)
- explicit success criteria.

The outer circle of students have pre-planned questions (see page 50). They might notice a change of direction in their peers' arguments, which they may see as a good exploration of alternative viewpoints. They may also identify when their peers use concrete examples to support their arguments or explore opposing views before drawing conclusions about their own beliefs. You can also get the outer circle of students to metacognitively unpick the quality of the talk itself using Voice 21's oracy framework and by reflecting on your explicit ground rules. The circle can make notes during the discussion and feedback can be provided verbally, with you facilitating this with guided questioning.

Case study

Fred (he/him), ECT, Brislington, Bristol

I wanted to encourage exploratory talk in my classroom and teach more dialogically, but my students weren't very good at engaging. I started by introducing the topic (we were looking at the play of Malorie Blackman's *Noughts & Crosses*) and then put students in groups and asked them to discuss the ideas. They erupted into noise and when I circulated the room, I realised the discussions weren't productive. When I was observed, I realised through discussion of the issues that this was because I hadn't set any ground rules or structured the talk to be purposeful. My lead practitioner told me to set the rules for discussion, then have a Socratic circle in my next lesson. This would enable us to collaboratively understand the ground rules and, afterwards, to reflect on how they had made the discussion more valuable.

Establishing the ground rules for the discussion at the start meant that I could remind students of them when they were carrying out the task, to keep them on track. They had a greater understanding of what made quality talk and so were actually happy to engage in the activity, which was much more structured through Socratic talk. Reminding them that they were talking about talk and evaluating the success of their discussions seemed to motivate them further. My lead practitioner observed that giving them planned questions not only helped to structure their discussions and allowed them to assess how well they followed the ground rules in the discussion, it also gave them the tools to be constructively critical of the quality of the talk, improving their practice for next time.

Fred used a handout, like this one, to structure his Socratic circle:

Name		Date
Highlight the questions you hear.	Why do you think that? Could you explain further? Could you give me an example? How do you feel about this? **Clarify**	What exceptions are there to this? Please can you explain why/how? Is this always the case? **Challenge**
How else could you answer that question? Who might see this differently? Why? **Exploring alternatives**	 **Noughts and Crosses**	Where is this evidenced in the story? Can you give me an example of that? How do you know this? **Using evidence**
What other questions could I ask? Why is this question important? Am I making sense? Why not? **Questioning the question**	Why is X important? What are the implications of X? **Consider consequences**	Note down the behaviours you think work well in this discussion:

Figure 3.2: Socratic questioning handout

Reflection

- How might your ground rules support success criteria in discussion?
- Decide what the ground rules will be for your next in-class discussion. Think about how you can make these rules explicit to students.
- How might a Socratic circle support you in creating a more dialogic and exploratory classroom?

Encouraging students to reflect on their learning verbally really helps them to understand where they are and where they need to be. What has gone well? Do they feel they have achieved success in the task? Socratic talk is a great tool for structuring this kind of self-assessment.

Enriching discussion and developing reasoning

Students arrive in the classroom with a variety of experiences of talk at home, and it is at school that they have the best chance of developing the full repertoire of oracy skills. So, it is important to give students plenty of opportunity for speaking and listening. Alexander's 'talk moves' of discussing and arguing can be useful here. Exploring and discussing ideas with other people will enhance students' ability to think alone, and a rich and varied experience of language is key to developing individual thinking skills.

Mercer (2008) outlines several key elements of a good discussion. These can be adapted and summarised to apply to exploratory talk as follows:

1. Share appropriate information.
2. Reason critically and constructively.
3. Give concrete examples for ideas.
4. Ensure that everyone participates.
5. Check understanding through questioning.
6. Build on others' responses.
7. Strive for agreement.
8. Reflect on the talk process.

One way of ensuring effective discussion and clear reasoning is to use the reciprocal reading roles you looked at in Chapter 2:

- Predictor: Decides what the text is about/what might happen next.
- Questioner: Asks questions of the text at both sentence level and whole-text level.
- Clarifier: Ensures all meanings are understood.
- Summariser: Reflects on the learning from the text and summarises new knowledge.

Palincsar and Brown (1984) believe that these stages in what they call 'reciprocal teaching' increase comprehension, as the student becomes the teacher and takes on one of these roles.

Let's apply this theory of reciprocal reading to *Noughts & Crosses*.

Predictor		**Questioner**
• What is the text about? • What is suggested by the heading/pictures? • What does this line suggest?		• What does it mean to be a Cross? How does that differ from being a Nought? • How is identity important?
Clarifier		**Summariser**
• What does this word mean? • What is the meaning of this abstract language?	**Noughts and Crosses**	• How well has the group stuck to the ground rules? • What are the main points this group discussed?

Figure 3.3: Reciprocal reading in action

You can use your summarisers as the main point of communication between you and their group but change the summariser in each lesson. Ask them to reflect on the quality of talk within their group's discussion, considering the eight elements of good discussion on the previous page and giving feedback to the group on how they fulfilled their reciprocal roles. This will move groups into more symmetrical talk (that between student and student) and enable you to make lessons more student-led, with you in the role of facilitator. Make sure you give students an appropriate amount of discussion time for the task and allow some structured time for feedback at the end to encourage reflection.

Think-pair-share

I find the process of think-pair-share an easy way to ensure effective exploratory talk and I encourage my trainees to use this technique every time they give students new information.

First, allow students some thinking time to process what has been said. Then, ask them to speak to their 'turn and talk' partner. You can give them some directed questions or tell them what you would like them to feed back on. Once they have discussed their ideas for a couple of minutes, call on students at random (don't ask for hands up) to see what they think of the new information, probing and developing their ideas through questioning in a development towards Alexander's extending/elaborating 'talk move'. This will give students more confidence to respond, and will encourage them to feel accountable for their responses. It's an opportunity for them to discuss the material and make some reasoned judgements about it, as well as to practise their quality talk in a low-stakes way.

Challenge through questions

The next stage of the schema is 'Challenge', which can be enhanced by Alexander's 'talk moves' of questioning, extending and arguing. In reflection sessions with trainees, I often find that we talk for long periods about the quality of questioning in the lesson. Although a huge amount of the skill of questioning comes from being in the moment and thinking on your feet, it's useful to script questions in advance as part of your lesson planning. Using a layered question matrix when planning your lesson can help you probe and respond at the right level.

We're going to focus on four types of questions here:
* closed – requiring a definitive answer
* open – any answer can be valid (within reason!)
* leading – encouraging students to a desired answer
* expansive – guiding students towards a developed response with concrete examples.

The questions aim to:
* initiate – to recall or to elicit facts, reasons, ideas or opinions
* probe – to seek justification for an answer; to identify areas of agreement/disagreement
* expand – to seek out alternatives, to explore what the answer/idea is linked to, or to predict what might happen next.

(Alexander, 2020)

Here is an example of some questions from a layered question matrix.

Word level/ recall – opinion	Closed	What does X mean?	What is the difference between X and X?	What does this metaphor mean?	What do you observe in X?
Text level/seek justification	Open	Why might X have used X word?	How does X link to the idea of power?	Why has this tenor and vehicle been chosen?	Which is more important, X or X?
	Leading	Does X change the tone of the piece?	Does X support patriarchal ideas?	Have you heard these before?	Are there any patterns in X?
Context level/ alternatives; prediction	Expansive	How is language affecting the reader?	How might you apply this idea to your writing?	Could you apply this metaphor to anything else?	What might you conclude about the impact of X?

You might find it useful to consolidate comprehension using closed questions in a cold-call method first. Then you can develop the skill with more open, leading and expansive questioning to extend and argue. As a general rule, closed questions start with 'What is...?' and expansive questions generally start with 'How might...?'

When planning your lesson, start with the questions. You can use the template in the following task as a guide.

Task

Think about a lesson you are teaching this week and the skills you want to develop. Copy the table. Start by planning the questions.

Text/information:	Skills:
Closed (word level/recall – opinion)	What is...?
Open and leading (text level/seek justification)	Why might...? How does...? Where have...? Why might...?
Expansive (context level/ alternatives; prediction)	How might...? Who does...? What else might...?

After the lesson, try noting down some of the answers that students gave to your questions, and reflect on how you responded to the students in the moment. Did you respond with another question? Did it probe them further? Did it elicit an alternative viewpoint? Did the whole class understand? How do you know?

Concur: Moving to agreement through elaboration

The next stage of the pedagogical schema is 'Concur'. According to Mercer, all talk should ideally reach some form of agreement, and you can approach this using Alexander's 'talk moves' of arguing and extending. This is where you ensure that students have the knowledge they need to explore the text in more detail, encouraging them to think about and build on their answers to the initial questions.

Building consensus is important and depends on a number of factors:
- a clear debate
- contributions from all
- focusing and listening
- collective decisions.

Having regular debates in the classroom is a good way for students to work through the process of reaching agreement or conclusions through talk. Debate allows students to think in the moment and encourages them to respond eloquently and effectively, which are essential skills beyond school.

When planning debates and discussions, remember that the content is as important as the structure of the task. Debating motions that encourage students to think in depth about real-world issues is very important, as is choosing topics that support students in their specific context.

You can ensure the factors for consensus listed on the previous page are in place when defining the motion for debate with students. First, select a subject for a topical debate, such as the news that France wants to ban pictures of children on social media (this may need to be sensitively introduced). The move has been opposed by an English 'influencer' who sees her child as a star and has 'no regrets' about posting her life on social media (Northcott, *The Sunday Times*, 12 March 2023). Give students a copy of the article with some active reading questions (see Chapter 4), then ask them to debate a motion in groups of three, using some elaboration ideas. This process will support their critical exploration of the topic and prepare them for writing a discursive response in their GCSE English Language exam.

The motion might be: 'This house believes that photographs of children should be banned from social media.' You would then work to define the motion with the groups of three. Start by asking students to imagine a world where this motion has passed. Ask them to describe it to you. Use these elaboration questions as a guide:

- **What...** is meant by the motion?
- **How...** will this look if it's passed?
- **Who...** will it impact?
- **How far...** will the changes reach? (extent)

Throughout, students can elaborate on their ideas by focusing on the effects of the motion being passed:

- Political: Would this be a good political reform?
- Economic: How might this impact the economy?
- Social: Is there a moral argument here? How would different communities be affected? Is there any discrimination here?

To move to 'concur', students can build upon and challenge one another's arguments. After the debate, use a poll to assess whether consensus has been reached.

Responding to the response

You can pose pre-scripted questions in cold-call, and either correct or accept student responses. However, in order to probe and elaborate, you need to ask developmental questions. Developing ideas in question and response depends on two things: having enough subject knowledge and being really confident in your responses to students. It is important to develop students' thinking and for you as a teacher to feel empowered to follow the explorations wherever they might go, encouraging personal responses to the content from students. It is also important to listen intently in order to respond appropriately to the information and ideas that students may share.

So, how does this 'response to response' work in practice?

Content:	Chinonyerem Odimba's *Princess and The Hustler*
What does Phyllis's imaginary world suggest?	
Student response	Teacher questions to probe and encourage elaboration
She wishes to escape the harsh realities of the racial tensions in Bristol. She is redefining what is beautiful and making it apply to her life.	Based on what X said, how could we view X?
	If what X said is true, what implications does that have for X?
	What do you think of X idea?
	Could you explain this further?
	How did you come to this conclusion?
	Can you elaborate on that to help me understand?
	Does this link to anything else we have read?

As always, it's a good idea to plan your questions before the lesson. Pre-empting what students might say about a topic means you can be sure you are prompting them appropriately and in a truly dialogic, continuous way. Persistence is key to ensuring that quality talk prevails, so keep at it, set the ground rules, and plan ahead!

> **Reflection**
> - How do your ground rules permeate your ideas for talk in the classroom?
> - How can you use the question matrix to ensure that you are asking the right questions?
> - How might you use debate to move to 'concur'?
> - What questions might you pre-plan to respond to the response?

Reflect: Allowing for metacognitive review

Students need time to reflect on the quality of their talk and on what they have learned through the talk process. This can come through metacognitive elements of talk: a discussion of learning. I recently observed a lesson where the introduction of universal free school meals in primary schools was debated with a group of students from Tottenham in London. They were engaged and also refreshingly critical of the need for celebrities to get involved, believing that the government should be addressing the important issue of food poverty.

The task was structured as a balloon debate, which starts with a certain number of students (in this case, four) who put forward their arguments, then the best of those remain in the 'balloon'. Note that this kind of debate should not be pitched as a competition in which students 'lose' the argument and have to leave the debate, but as a collation of ideas during which two of the four original members become observers and reflect on the debate in much the same style as the Socratic circle. The original four put forward their arguments, and eventually two of them move to become evaluators of the debate. Timing the activity is important, and using a visual timer will add urgency and pace.

Here's a quick summary of how it works:
- Students discuss their ideas in groups of four: two proposing and two opposing the motion. Make sure you set out clear, specific success criteria, such as:
  - Put forward a clear argument.
  - Explore alternative views.
  - Use engaging language and structure.
  - Give concrete examples for ideas.
  - Accept and respond to challenges.
- You can probe students to agree, develop or challenge one another's arguments as you circulate the groups, supporting them with sentence stems written on the board if necessary. Groups can then decide through a vote which side is strongest in line with the success criteria and, after collating their best arguments, one member of the stronger team becomes the summariser. The summariser is important and decides the quality of the debate, based on Oracy Cambridge and Voice 21's oracy framework and the ground rules. It is vital to emphasise the importance of the summariser role so students feel valued and integral to the development of their group's debate.
- Group members then decide who they want to speak for each side. One of the other students leaves the balloon to become the clarifier. Their job is to ensure that there is clarity in all the responses (working with the summariser) and that the quality of rebuttal is high. Rebuttal means responding directly to challenges, which helps students to develop their own arguments in light of these. The clarifier creates statements for rebuttal from the opposing team's arguments and the group practises responding to these.

- The end of the debate comes with questions (or points of interest) from the students outside the balloon. The summariser and the clarifier can work together to ensure that these are probing and challenge the speakers, perhaps using the question matrix. The students also assess the quality of the response.
- You can repeat the exercise with a new motion and with students swapping roles to give all students the opportunity to perform.

In this example, all groups had the same motion, but you could give each group of four a different motion to discuss and then include a follow-up lesson where you provide success criteria for the clarifier to refer to in order to evaluate the quality of their debate.

Consolidation and targeted practice

To continue with the metacognitive element of reflection, I like to embed a number of consolidation exercises in order to assess students' learning in talk. While I often have short writing tasks in my repertoire, I also like to use plenaries in the form of verbal peer assessment. You could consolidate a talk-focused lesson by sharing the question matrix with students, allowing them to track their thought processes and identify any changes in their thinking throughout the discussions or debates you have facilitated.

Developing talk can also come through asking students to 'express it better'. Of course, it's essential to value their initial ideas and their own culture of expression, but building on these by adding specific structure to their talk can enhance their eloquence of expression. We will look at the technicalities of this in Chapter 5, but here's a good consolidation exercise for 'express it better'.

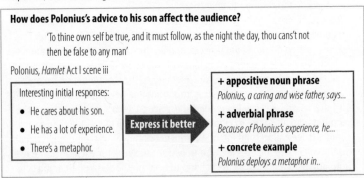

How does Polonius's advice to his son affect the audience?

'To thine own self be true, and it must follow, as the night the day, thou cans't not then be false to any man'

Polonius, *Hamlet* Act I scene iii

Interesting initial responses:
- He cares about his son.
- He has a lot of experience.
- There's a metaphor.

Express it better

+ appositive noun phrase
Polonius, a caring and wise father, says...

+ adverbial phrase
Because of Polonius's experience, he...

+ concrete example
Polonius deploys a metaphor in..

Figure 3.4: 'Express it better' in action

Effective oracy depends on **non-declarative knowledge**, which supports the sensory and connection elements of communication. But how do we refine this? The answer is through targeted practice.

Practice depends on isolating specific skills to improve. Building on Oracy Cambridge and Voice 21's oracy framework, we can generate success criteria for oracy, targeting specific skills for improvement.

Words	Rhetorical features	Ideas	Structure	Use of argument	Listen and respond
Use engaging vocabulary.	Include persuasive features.	Include engaging, relevant ideas.	Ensure ideas are structured in an engaging manner.	Give reasons and evidence for your ideas.	Respond perceptively; elaborate/ challenge.
Intonation	**Clarity of expression**	**Projection**	**Eye contact/ confidence**	**Use of non-verbals**	**Collaboration**
Vary the pattern of language to engage.	Speak slowly and articulately.	Use voice powerfully and clearly.	Make confident eye contact; present self in confident manner.	Integrate effective body language, gesture and stance to engage.	Question effectively

Task

Assess the success of oracy in your classroom. Choose an activity in which you would like to use talk. Using the oracy framework from the start of this chapter, assess your students on the quality of their communication. Give them a mark out of 5 for each section. Use this as an indicator of which part of the oracy framework you might focus on for each of your teaching groups.

Talk task (select one)	Cognitive	Linguistic	Physical	Social and emotional
	/5	/5	/5	/5
Speech or Group discussion or Paired exploration	How well does their content suit their purpose? Do students question the ideas well? Have they organised their talk coherently? Have they made valid judgements?	How engaging is their language? Does vocabulary enhance their speech? Have they used the right tone?	How well do they project their voice? Is there clarity in their speech? Are they using non-verbal gestures effectively? How is their posture? Do they make effective eye contact?	Do they listen to others? Do they respond effectively? Is there an awareness of audience? How well do they collaborate?

Using the schema to scaffold oracy

The schema offers a scaffold to ensure that oracy interventions are sustained. Making sure that all students are engaged through a hook and through active listening practice will secure participation and development. Knowing their boundaries and understanding the ground rules will secure every student's contribution, which will in turn allow them all to explore ideas and information. Setting up questions, debate and opportunities to argue will not only challenge them in talk, but also encourage them to initiate challenge themselves. This can all lead to a potential consensus and, ultimately, to meaningful reflection and discussion about their learning.

Strategies and takeaways

- **Lend me your ears:** Making listening an explicit skill will support and engage all students in their oracy.
- **Use the schema:** This will help you structure talk and is a useful basis for success criteria in communication.
- **Make the rules explicit**: Exploratory talk needs explicit ground rules.
- **Keep talking:** Dialogic teaching includes 'talk moves'; discussing, questioning, extending (or elaborating) and arguing all support students' development.
- **Check what they've learned and ask them to express it better:** Talk must be consolidated to assess progress. It is not always essential to talk like a writer in English classrooms, but there are always ways to improve expression.
- **Practice makes perfect**: Oracy is enhanced by targeted practice.

Chapter 4: Inspiring reading

Why read?

Reading is the English teacher's bread and butter – and probably one of the main reasons you chose to teach this subject. The research in this chapter focuses on the benefits of reading for pleasure, and it will help you to structure reading interventions in the classroom to help students gain a real joy from reading.

As the Department for Education (May 2012) notes, the benefits of reading for pleasure are wide-ranging. It increases reading attainment in class as well as writing ability; it also improves text comprehension and grammar, and broadens vocabulary. It encourages positive reading attitudes and greater confidence as a reader, and establishes a habit that can continue through later life. In addition, reading for pleasure enhances general knowledge, ensures community participation, and helps students to develop a better understanding of other cultures and even a greater insight into human nature and decision-making.

Ofsted's Reading Framework (July 2023) also offers a number of reasons why reading is key to development in all aspects of life, noting most importantly that if students can't read well, they are unable to access the rest of the curriculum. In her exploration of reading for pleasure, Cremin (2020) found that students who read make strong cognitive progress in both vocabulary and mathematics between the ages of 10 and 16. Reading can also be considered an art form. Frier (1985) notes that 'teaching kids to read and write should be an artistic event' and that 'many teachers work bureaucratically when they should work artistically'. Finally, reading for pleasure can be seen as a tool for working towards social justice, inclusively engaging all students in diverse texts. (The Collins anthology *Who We Are: 24 brilliant texts to enrich your KS3 English curriculum* offers some great ideas for diverse texts that will engage your students.)

To allow students access to all these benefits, we must ensure that they are well supported to develop their reading skills in the classroom.

The landscape for reading for pleasure doesn't look too good. The National Literacy Trust (2023) found that around 2 in 5 young people aged 8–18 (43.4%) said they enjoyed reading in their spare time. Of those who received free school meals, 39.5% said they enjoyed the pursuit, which suggests that advantage is a key factor in access to reading that develops into reading for pleasure. Only 52.9% said that their parents encouraged them to read, highlighting the need for better reading environments for young people, such as access to libraries. When I worked in schools as a literacy lead, I created mini libraries in each classroom – an area to simply enjoy books. You might consider doing the same if you have the space in your classroom.

Cremin has already suggested some ways in which these issues may be tackled. She explores the change in the definition of reading since 2000 according to the OECD, noting that we now recognise the motivational and behavioural characteristics of reading alongside cognitive characteristics (OECD, 2019). However, we do not seem to have made a noticeable change in supporting students to love reading since 2019. It is important to acknowledge and develop skills beyond comprehension, decoding and making judgements about texts. Cremin argues that 'to create such communities [of readers] teachers need rich repertoires of children's texts, knowledge of the young readers, a responsive pedagogy and an understanding of reading'.

Let's look at how these strategies could be embedded in your teaching of reading.

Pedagogical schema for reading

Below is an example schema for reading. Embedding this into your practice will support students' reading so they become more inclined to read for pleasure and benefit from all the advantages that brings.

Reading	Predict	Respond and elaborate	Infer	Explore	Judge
	Set predictive activities on the text.	Ask questions to secure comprehension. Ask questions that get students thinking across and beyond the text.	Explore abstract ideas.	Make connections beyond the text.	Summarise understanding through evaluation.

This schema is based on Graves and Graves' seminal research into the Scaffolded Reading Experience (SRE) (2003), which has become so well-established since it was introduced in 1994 that you may have experienced it as a student yourself. It includes three stages:

- pre-reading (making predictions)
- during reading (chunking reading, questioning)
- post-reading (creating grids and tables, quotation 'explosions').

The 'Predict' section of the schema is part of the pre-reading stage; 'Respond and elaborate', 'Infer' and 'Explore' are a mix of during reading and post-reading; 'Judge' occurs in the post-reading stage. All three stages of the SRE and the six stages of the schema above use a combination of teaching modes, including **didactic**, dialogic, collaborative (student talk) and independent.

As you work through the schema and implement reading strategies in your classroom, remember that students will always benefit from hearing how a text *should* be read. Take every opportunity to read aloud to your students. Some ideas for how you might do this are included below.

Predict: Getting ready to read

It is important to 'chunk' the reading process for students so that it doesn't seem overwhelming. Reading is a complex process that relies on different parts of the brain, and pre-reading support will help students to better manage the cognitive load.

The 'Predict' stage of the schema might involve:

- recapping prior knowledge
- teaching new concepts or words
- setting a focus for the reading.

Recapping prior knowledge

A short review of learning works well as part of a starter activity. Students never read texts discretely – they are always bringing something of their prior knowledge to the table, whether it's contextual knowledge, opinions, prejudices or personal experience. It's impossible to summarise all their knowledge into a single set of questions, but it's essential to make the retrieval of prior knowledge explicit. For example, imagine you were reading the following introduction to a non-fiction text:

> *This 1894 article details the wedding of Czar Nicholas II of Russia to Princess Alexandra, which took place in St Petersburg. Their wedding was brought forward because Nicholas's father died, making Nicholas*

ruler of Russia. This extract reports on people getting ready to watch the procession, and their reaction once the wedding has finished.

You might ask the following questions to access students' prior knowledge and understanding:

- What kind of content do articles have?
- What do you know about 'czars' and 'princesses'?
- Where is St Petersburg?
- What do you know about 1894 or the 1890s?
- What do you know about weddings?
- What do you know about succession?
- What do you know about people's reaction to royalty?

It is important to develop a mental model to explore prior knowledge so that students can reproduce this thinking in an exam – or just enjoy reading outside their English lessons. The process could be summarised as:

- What is the text type? What might that include?
- What is the main topic here? What do I know about that topic?
- When was this written? What do I know about that time?
- Which people/characters are in the text? What do I know about them?
- What reactions are mentioned? What might they suggest?

You can summarise this as:

Type $\rightarrow$ topic $\rightarrow$ time $\rightarrow$ character $\rightarrow$ response

Activating prior knowledge makes accessing the text much easier. It avoids the temptation for students to 'feature-spot' (for example, looking for metaphors in a text with no idea of its wider meaning) or to read texts in isolation. Students do not need a lot of new knowledge to understand a text, but making links to existing background knowledge will allow them to explore the significance of themes and ideas when they read.

Teaching new concepts or words

Imagine you are preparing to read an extract from a text with your class as part of a comprehension exercise. For example, students might be learning about owls and their attributes. They will be using the skills of decoding, blending, word recognition, fluency, prosody, comprehension and inference that they learned at primary school. At secondary level, expectations for reading are expanded to include analysis and evaluation. To assist students to meet this extra challenge, the pre-reading work can help students to reach a secure understanding of the text, for example by supporting them to decipher unfamiliar vocabulary or by prompting them to think about what associations a word or image might bring to mind. For instance, the owl may be described in the text as having 'percipience'

– a noun meaning the quality of having insight or complete understanding. This is something they could attribute to the owl before they read to support them in understanding the new vocabulary in this sentence:

> *Landing silently on the branch, the owl rapidly scanned its*
> *surroundings, its percipience evident to the entire forest.*

When you get to your actual reading, you want students to be able to explore and infer what this might represent. They also need to identify the pronouns and understand that this astuteness refers to the sentence's subject. To ensure that students are prepared to make some evaluative comments about the owl with this new and more complex vocabulary, you could start by highlighting more complex words or phrases and isolating these prior to reading to support the 'Predict' process.

Word blasts

A good activity when introducing students to new vocabulary is the 'word blast', which activates prior learning and builds connections. It is adapted from the Frayer model (1969), which helps to identify unfamiliar concepts in vocabulary by defining them and exploring examples and non-examples (knowing what the concept *isn't* supports definition).

You could structure a word blast using a grid like the one on the next page, working through it with your class. Model the start of the activity and then leave the boxes empty for students to complete as a starter activity before reading a text. The more you use the word blast, the more automated the process will become for students as they develop a mental model of imagining words, which will help them make judicious use of their newly learnt vocabulary.

On the next page is an example of a completed word blast grid for 'percipience'. You could show to students five minutes after they have started their own empty grids to help them.

Definition	Antonyms	Connotations
having sensitive insight or comprehension; perceptiveness	incomprehension; misperception	wisdom, owls, foreshadowing, astuteness
	Non examples	
	I am a very percipience person. *(used incorrectly as an adjective instead of noun)*	
	If a student keeps trying, it shows their percipience.	
	(used incorrectly to mean persistence)	
Where have you heard the word?		**Image**
A teacher may use it to describe a student's astute response. It could be attributed to a wise person.	**percipience** *Word class: noun*	
When might you use it?	**How might you use it?**	**Etymology (where does the word come from?)**
It can be used in descriptive or non-fiction writing.	*Landing silently on the branch, the owl rapidly scanned its surroundings, its percipience evident to the entire forest.*	Latin origin – from *per* meaning 'entirely' + *capere* meaning 'take' = to seize or understand.

Figure 4.1: A word blast

Image antonyms

I recently observed a trainee English teacher using images effectively to support understanding of new vocabulary before a reading task. He asked his class to decode the meaning of the words using visual images to represent the word and its antonym. The following example shows how you might do this for the word 'tangible'. It enables students not only to understand the meaning of the word when they come across it in a reading text, but also allows them to consider words that might have an opposite meaning.

tangible

intangible

Figure 4.2: Vocabulary: antonym pairs for the word 'tangible'

Setting a focus for the reading

As you prepare students to read a new text, use planned predictive questions and activities in order to explore new ideas and meanings in short extracts of the text itself. These pre-reading tasks will aid comprehension when students finally read the full text, as they offer an opportunity to preview themes and ideas or to make sure students understand an important point about context. Setting a focus for the reading will help to manage your students' cognitive load.

Imagine you are preparing your class to read the scene in *Macbeth* where Macbeth has killed Duncan and his hands are covered in blood. The focus you want to set for students is his feelings of guilt and how these manifest in the character. Pre-reading questions might centre on the feelings students should explore in their reading:

- Have you ever done something that has made you feel guilty?
- What kind of emotion is guilt?
- How does it make a person feel?

Linking the idea of guilt to personal experience allows for a more authentic response and allows students to think perceptively about the emotion. This is a stepping stone to an analytical reading of the extract, allowing them to consider the impact on Macbeth as a character more fully.

Using images to predict what might happen is another great way to set a focus for a reading text. Imagine you are reading *A Christmas Carol* with your class and want to recap previous knowledge as well as make predictions about how the story might develop. You could use a series of images, supplemented with planned questions about the narrative, to allow students to make predictions about the story.

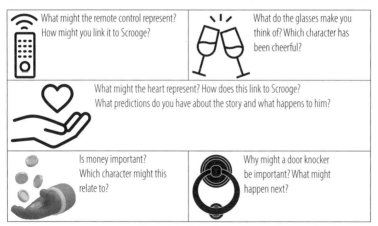

Figure 4.3: Using images to predict text development

You could also ask students to make predictions about the narrative using snippets of the upcoming chapter:

> ❝ *If they would rather die,' said Scrooge, 'they had better do it, and decrease the surplus population.* ❞

> ❝ *Darkness is cheap, and Scrooge liked it.* ❞

> ❝ *Mankind was my business.* ❞

> ❝ *I am here to-night to warn you, that you have yet a chance and hope of escaping my fate.* ❞

- How is Scrooge developing as a character here? How would you describe him? What is the importance of something being 'cheap'?
- Who might be talking about 'fate'? What might it be?
- What predictions can you make about the story based on this extract?

Case study

Andrew (he/him) – first year trainee, London

Some pre-reading of the text is a game changer – predicting what the text might be about <u>and</u> isolating some powerful quotations before reading really helps my students to pick up ideas and themes within the text when we read. It also supports the idea of 'text before knowledge' – immersing students in the experience of reading the text and scaffolding this with some questions allows for some engaging responses to the drama we have been reading.

There are other ways of setting a focus for your reading of a text using images and talk, too. Imagine your students are going to read and discuss the key ideas in Shelley's poem 'England in 1819', from the AQA GCSE English Literature poetry cluster *Worlds and Lives*.

England in 1819

An old. mad. blind. despised. and dying King;
Princes. the dregs of their dull race. who flow
Through public scorn. — mud from a muddy spring;
Rulers who neither see nor feel nor know.
But leechlike to their fainting country cling
Till they drop. blind in blood. without a blow.
A people starved and stabbed in th' untilled field;
An army. whom liberticide and prey
Makes as a two-edged sword to all who wield;
Golden and sanguine laws which tempt and slay;
Religion Christless. Godless — a book sealed;
A senate. Time's worst statute. unrepealed—
Are graves from which a glorious Phantom may
Burst. to illumine our tempestuous day.

By Percy Bysshe Shelley (1839)

Figure 4.4: Reading poetry

So that you can predict what the text might be about, ask students to decide what the three images suggest – what are their connotations? Based on the images, they may come up with ideas such as loyalty, pride, power, new beginnings, anger, residue, ghostliness, a parasite. These link directly to Shelley's belief that rulers don't care about their country and its problems – they are like parasites that die of overindulgence, but there is some hope that a redeeming spirit may rise to alleviate the difficulties of the times.

It is important to have in your mind the ideas you would like students to pick up on, in order to draw these out of the connotations you explore in class. For instance, they may think of a 'Phantom' as a comical idea, so you should guide them to seeing it as a restorative spirit, bringing enlightenment to England. However, to begin with, don't discourage students' interpretations – you can wait until the 'Respond and elaborate' stage of the schema for them to recognise whether their ideas are relevant.

When they come to the full read, you could develop this into active reading by asking students to match the images to concepts in the text (emphasise to them that any interpretation is valid). For example, they might link the flag in the picture of the soldier to the words, 'old, mad, despised and dying King' – a symbol of royalty perhaps ridiculed by Shelley, or to 'a people starved and stabbed' – a symbol of a community that displays loyalty and bravery on the battlefield. Either of these would be a valid link and would provide an opportunity to explore ideas of ambiguity in the poem.

You could also set up a talk activity to engage students before they read the poem. For example, you could give students short phrases from the poem, then write the following motion on the board and ask them to discuss it using the phrases.

Shelley has completely lost hope in his country.

For this, you could zoom in on the words in a word cloud like the one below, asking students which words link to hope and which seem to suggest that England is destitute. This will set them up to discuss the issues dialogically, engage them in the ideas of the poem and allow them to start thinking about the themes and ideas Shelley presents.

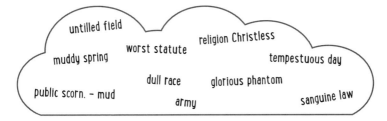

Respond and elaborate: Encouraging active reading

The next stage of the schema is 'Respond and elaborate'. This involves using questioning first to ensure that students have fully comprehended the text and then to encourage them to think more broadly, across and beyond the text. At this stage, students are actively involved in thinking about the text while reading, making them active readers. Active readers have a specific outcome from their reading – for example, if you're reading *A Monster Calls*, you may ask students to identify examples of symbolism while they read. This means they are actively involved in the process and have a tangible outcome in the form of examples of symbols.

'Just reading'

Some refreshing evidence has recently come to light about the power of 'just reading'. A 2018 report from the University of Sussex by Westbrook et al showed that simply reading challenging texts aloud at a faster pace, without interruptions to analyse or produce work based on the text, moved 'poorer readers' to be 'good' readers. By fully immersing themselves in reading, they are able to connect personally with the text, which allows an authentic response to it – something that McGeown et al. had suggested in 2016.

'Just reading' means a fast-paced read that is supported by teaching inference, unpicking difficult-to-read sections mid-text and creating reading groups to further support less confident readers. In a faster read, the text becomes more coherent, and reading is experienced as a 'collaboratively constructed, active and engaged process' (Westbrook et al., 2018)

The evidence for the benefits of 'just reading' highlights the following myths about first exposure to a text:

- Poorer readers needed simpler texts.
- Reading aloud equates to comprehension.
- Every part of a text needs to be analysed.
- Comprehension leads to inference.
- Teachers have to be in control of the reading.

The fact that all these points have been shown to be untrue opens up new ways of approaching reading texts in the classroom. For example, rather than finding different texts for more and less confident readers, the whole class can be set the same text. We can also select particular sections of a text to respond to in detail rather than the whole thing, and we can teach inference explicitly. Importantly, students can be given greater control over their own reading and be active participants in the process.

Responsive and elaborative reading

As experienced readers, we implicitly build a world in our minds through a process of questioning, response, clarification and elaboration. To help students reach a point where they also do this instinctively, it's important to demonstrate the process to them explicitly.

The 'during reading' stage outlined by Graves and Graves (2003) can either be teacher-led with limited stops (i.e. you should quickly clarify meaning where required, and focus on reading for pleasure) or through guided group reading. You might find it useful to look back at Palincsar and Brown's (1984) reciprocal reading model in Chapter 3. Here, students would take on the roles of predictor, clarifier, questioner and summariser to structure the read. You could give them prompts as below and pause mid-read for them to discuss, encouraging them to make notes in preparation.

Predictor	Clarifier	Questioner	Summariser
It seems that it might… I predict…	Are we all clear on what X means? Can I just clarify…	A question I have is… How might…?	To summarise… Thinking about what we have all said makes me think…

When reading with limited stops, the University of Sussex study suggests that teacher-led reading aloud has more impact than students reading, so try to lead the reading yourself to allow your students to hear a well-practised reader!

There are two aspects of active reading: responsive, to secure comprehension, and elaborative, to develop analysis and evaluation. Responsive questions can be surface level (Who is he? Where has he come from?). Elaborative questions can delve deeper to make connections across and beyond the text (Where have we met him before? How is he feeling now? What might happen next?)

Once you have read a text with your students, make sure that they have understood characters, events and ideas correctly (this is the 'Respond' stage of the schema). You can do this through questioning, re-reading and sharing definitions of words. You can also use scaffolded activities like the situation models below to draw out ideas about character motivations, helping students to add details to the imagined world they create as they read. Note that you can also stop and ask questions to check comprehension at an appropriate point part-way through the text, even with a fast-paced read, especially with more challenging passages.

Situation models

Situation models can be a useful way to secure students' comprehension of a text. Zwaan and Radvansky (1998) describe situation models as 'integrated mental representations of a described state of affairs'. That is, they represent the world that a text creates. Understanding this world and making connections across it supports students' understanding of the text itself.

Zwaan and Radvansky describe the following key elements that effective readers remember when they are reading fiction:
- what the protagonist does
- the time things happen
- the spatial elements of the story
- the causal relations between events
- the protagonist's aims and how events relate to these.

These elements can be reproduced in a different format – or situation model – from the original text.

After an initial reading, ask students to make notes about the characters and events. Remind them not to focus solely on the protagonist, but to think about all characters' motivations and how they link to themes. Get students to add to these notes throughout all lessons on the text. These notes then form the basis of the situation model they create, which is in a different format to the text itself.

A great way to format a situation model is through a storyboard or grid (see opposite), which you can use as a framework, adding detail about a text as you work through it. The finished grid is also a useful revision tool. You could base the grid on two things to do with the text: responding (including comprehension) and then elaborating.

Start by noting down the key events within the text. This can include a summary of the events, then questions to clarify what has happened and to explore motivations. The next stage is to explore further through elaborative questions, considering alternative ideas, how the text may be received, and the implications of events at a whole-text level. Ask students questions to clarify the text in respond – for example, *Where is the story set? What is meant by X?* – then develop this response through questioning: *What has prompted this action by X? What else has happened to this character?* Finally, encourage students to elaborate by completing the sentences – for example, *I predict that X will... There must be something we don't know, I think....*

Here is an example of a grid-format situation model for *An Inspector Calls* by J.B. Priestley.

	Key events	Respond	Elaborate
1	1912; the Birling family celebrates the engagement of daughter Sheila and Gerald Croft. Mr Birling is happy with this new connection, as it will bring 'higher prices' at his factory. The doorbell rings – it's a police inspector investigating the death of a young woman, Eva Smith.	What is an engagement? What social standing might a factory owner have? What else happened in 1912? (Content warning: suicide. Ensure you use a trigger warning for your class.)	Do you think that perhaps Sheila isn't very happy about this match, which appears to have been arranged?
2	Mr Birling sees a photograph of the girl – he fired her in 1910. Sheila also recalls an interaction with Eva, in which she had the girl sacked from a department store after Eva smirked when Sheila tried on a dress there. Sheila feels guilty. We learn that Eva changed her name to Daisy Renton. Now Gerald realises he also knew her – he had an affair with her.	What does 'smirk' mean? Why might this have an impact on the audience? How does Sheila's response differ from her father's? What does the difference between Birling's attitude and Sheila's tell us?	What is the dramatic impact of the photograph? Is this a patriarchal society? What freedom does Gerald have to have an affair?
3	Sheila gives her engagement ring back to Gerald. Mrs Birling confesses that she had contact with Eva, when Eva came to her charity. Eva was pregnant and called herself Mrs Birling. She asked for help, but was refused.	Why were engagements so important in 1912? Why did Mrs Birling find it so offensive that Eva used her name? Who might be the father of Eva's baby?	How does Mrs Birling's condemnation of the father add tension here?

	Key events	Respond	Elaborate
4	Eric, the Birlings' son, is revealed as the father of Eva's child. He stole money from Mr Birling to provide for Eva. Inspector Goole tells the family they are all to blame for the death of Eva/Daisy.	Why did Eric steal the money?	What do you know about guilt in relation to crimes? Has a crime been committed here? (Ensure you use a trigger warning for your class.)
5	After the inspector leaves, the family discusses the possibility that he may not have been a real police officer. They call the police and this is confirmed. Mr Birling, Mrs Birling and Gerald all congratulate themselves, upsetting Sheila and Eric.	What does the characters' 'relief' tell us about them? Why might Priestley use a fake inspector?	Have you ever experienced a different response from older and younger generations?
6	The phone rings. A girl has just died and the police are on their way.	Why might the police be coming to the Birlings? What dramatic device signals a change in this scene?	What do you think will happen to the family?

Figure 4.5: Example adaptation of the situation model

DARTs

Another useful reading strategy to help students respond to and elaborate on a text is Lunzer and Gardner's directed activities related to text (DARTs) (1984). These activities can take several formats, including:

- text completion (gap-fill)
- diagram completion
- table completion
- restructuring text (putting events in the correct order)
- annotating or highlighting
- chunking text
- creating diagrams such as quotation explosions
- creating tables.

There is some overlap between DARTs and situational models. For example, the grid above could be seen as a table completion DART.

Let's look at an example of a DART – chunking the text – based on a non-fiction article about how critics were being paid by filmmakers to boost ratings on the film review website Rotten Tomatoes. Here students *respond* to the text by deciphering an idea about the content and *elaborate* on these ideas by making connections to their prior knowledge. This allows them to see the diversity of opinion within non-fiction texts and come up with a well-supported argument in response to it. Students read the article and then, with support from you, come up with a thesis statement based on the information they have read. They then 'chunk' the text, reading it in smaller chunks and finding arguments for and against their thesis. To make this a really active process, you could alternatively give them a standpoint on the article before they read and ask them to select evidence for and against as they read.

Thesis statement:	Rotten Tomatoes is an important authentic rating scheme for films, so it must be protected and not corrupted by payment.
For	**Against**
'Many people use the website to determine whether to see films.'	'It can be overloaded with opinion and deter some viewers from seeing movies that they may enjoy.'

We'll return to DARTs in the later stages of the schema, as they're equally useful in the post-reading phases.

Task

Choose a non-fiction article you will be teaching and decide on a thesis statement that could be made based on the arguments within it. Decide on one argument for and one against and then prepare a text-chunking task to use with your class using the template above.

Summarising learning from the text is very important and should not be rushed. I like to ask students to reflect on their reading and to rank the importance of their new learning. For example, after reading a new scene from *Romeo and Juliet*, students may have learned three new things about Romeo. I would ask them to rank these in importance when considering Romeo as the protagonist.

Reflection

- Could you integrate a fast-paced 'just reading' approach in your classes?
- How could you consolidate learning from a text in your classroom?
- What texts are you teaching soon that you could support with responsive and elaborative reading techniques?
- Which DARTs might you use to support your students in the 'during reading' phase?

Infer: Understanding abstract meaning

The 'Infer' stage of the schema is the first of the post-reading phases – that is, it's the next step after students have done an initial read and you're sure they have a solid understanding of the text. Put simply, inference is reading between the lines. Making inferences about a text is key to developing students' ability to express what they have learned, as well as considering how they might explore their new knowledge through literary reasoning. Inferences are based on delving deeper into the text and understanding abstract meaning – that is, students need to consider ideas theoretically. The kind of sentences you want students to be able to complete through inference are:

- Beauty is explored in the text by...
- The overarching idea of truth is exposed in...
- Resentment is further portrayed through...

It is useful to get students thinking metacognitively about the text they have read. You can trigger this with certain questions. For example:

- What has changed in your thinking from what you predicted about the text?
- What do you know now that you didn't know at the start of this lesson?
- Are there any further questions we need to ask?

Ask students to add any new information or events to their situation model if they have started one.

Look at the following extract from *Romeo and Juliet*, in which Romeo addresses Friar Laurence. Imagine that students have completed pre-reading activities to define some of the difficult vocabulary and set a focus for the reading. You have asked appropriate questions to secure their comprehension of the extract and to elaborate on their understanding. Now, you want students to really think about the tone of the piece and to explore the overarching ideas of the text, taking the first steps towards analysis and evaluation.

> ❛ *Be merciful, say 'death'.*
> *For exile hath more terror in his look,*
> *Much more than death...*
> *How hast thou the heart,*
> *Being a divine, a ghostly confessor,*
> *A sin-absolver, and my friend profess'd,*
> *To mangle me with that word 'banished'?* ❜

You could read the scene with the class, then write a list of questions on the board to help students reflect on their response to the extract. For example:

- If you were to set these lines of Romeo's to music, what song might you choose?

- How would you define the mood of this scene? What words make you feel like that?
- How is language used to express Romeo's deteriorating relationship with the Friar?
- A critic thinks there is a pervading feeling of resentment here. Do you agree?
- What alternative interpretations of the mood of the piece might there be?

Encourage students to use concrete examples from the text in their responses, but also to make their own interpretations. It can be useful to explore those personal interpretations in further class discussion. You might also consider providing students with an alternative point of view (cognitive conflict), which helps to develop literary reasoning.

> **Reflection**
> - How can you support your students to explore abstract meaning?

Teaching figurative language – abstract to concrete

❛ *It is the East, and Juliet is the sun.* ❜

Figurative language links to abstract meaning and to fully understand it, students need to rely on their inferential skills. An effective way to teach metaphors and similes is through exposing their three parts:
- the tenor: the thing the writer is trying to describe to the reader (Juliet)
- the vehicle: the imaginative idea it is compared with to help the audience understand it (the sun) – this is the 'made up' bit and it is important for students to understand that this is abstract
- the ground: the things that the tenor and the vehicle have in common (bright, beautiful, life-giving).

Task

Romeo and Juliet is an excellent play to use to explore metaphor in more depth. Choose one of the quotations below and carry out a 'comparison alley' activity to label the three parts and explore the similarities and differences between the tenor and the vehicle. The 'alley' is the ground – what do the concrete thing and the abstract idea have in common? This runs down the middle of the visual you use with your class like an alley.

> ❛ I talk of dreams,
> Which are the children of an idle brain,
> Begot of nothing but vain fantasy ❜
>
> (Act I, Scene 4, lines 97–99)

> ❛ O happy dagger,
> This is thy sheath. There rust and let me die. ❜
>
> (Act V, Scene 3, lines 183–184)

Tenor (the subject)	Ground (What do they have in common?)	Vehicle (What is the 'made-up' part?)
Juliet's body		The dagger's sheath

Kispal (2008) states that 'some children fail to draw what might seem like obvious inferences while others introduce ideas that seem entirely irrelevant', so it is important to guide students between the two extremes by ensuring they understand the 'ground' – the things the tenor and vehicle have in common.

Rose (2016) explores the different 'levels' of reading. He believes that reading starts with *decoding* – looking for letter patterns in words. Readers then look for *literal* meaning within the sentence. They then move to *inferential* reading – reading across the text – before finally reading *interpretively* – beyond the text. Rose states that inference comes from zooming in and doing a close read of shorter passages after first reading a full text.

The following example shows how you could use planned questioning about a text to move from decoding and literal understanding to an inferential exploration of meaning in shorter extracts. It's based on a non-fiction text dating from 1852 about the importance of tea-drinking to British society.

This wondrous beverage seems actually endowed with the most opposite properties; it warms us in winter and refreshes us in summer; soothes and yet stimulates; fits us equally for action or repose. Born in the land of silk and cotton, it forms with them a truly illustrious trio; but though the youngest of the three, it is the greatest favourite, and is a welcome guest with millions to whom its associates are strangers.

From an article in *The Leisure Hour*, 1852

Literal questions:

- What do the words 'wondrous', 'endowed' and 'repose' mean?
- Where might the land of silk and cotton be?

Inferential questions:

- What impression does the phrase 'the land of silk and cotton' give you about tea?
- What language device does the writer use in the phrases 'the youngest of the three' and 'a welcome guest'?
- What impression does the idea of having 'associates' give?

Interpretative questions:

- What is your experience of tea?
- Does your own experience link to this description? If so, in what way?
- What do you know about who grows and produces tea, and where it is grown and produced? What do you know about the production of tea in the Victorian era?

Kispal's research found the need for students to be active participants in reading. She also believes that background knowledge is important in forming inferences so it is essential to unlock students' prior knowledge and help them to make connections during the pre-reading stage of the schema. The study revealed that questioning was an important aspect of developing inference skills in the classroom and teachers should ask 'How do you know?' when students make inferences; however, this questioning should take place after reading, to support the benefit of 'just reading' first. Students should also be encouraged to ask 'why' questions themselves and to generate their own questions about a text. Chris Curtis's teacher pack, *Develop Brilliant Reading* (2022), explores some interesting types of inferential reading based on Kispal's research.

Task

Choose some imagery that you might want to explore, or use the following example from *Dr Jekyll and Mr Hyde*:

> *with ape-like fury, he was trampling his victim underfoot*

Ask students to make some inferences about meaning by exploring the connotations of the words and images chosen and comparing them to the ground. Zoom in on relevant inferences after a discussion, and prompt students to ask 'why' questions of the evidence. Draw a blank version of this grid on your board to fill in with students.

Tenor	Ground	Vehicle	Connotations	'Why' questions
Mr Hyde	Unfeeling Dangerous Inhuman	'ape-like' 'trampling'	strong animalistic	Why was Mr Hyde out at night? Why might Mr Hyde have this kind of temper?

Quotation explosions

Quotation explosions – another of Lunzer and Gardner's DARTs – are an effective way for students to explore and structure inference in a text. The technique encourages students to make sense of texts and build connections, and it prepares them well for analytical writing.

The following is a worked example of a quotation explosion using a quotation from Liz Berry's poem 'Homing'.

1. What does the line mean? She tries to hide her accent but sometimes it 'escapes'.	2. What are the connotations of the key words? • 'escape': constrained, strength, wily • 'guttural': distinctive; throaty; husky • 'saft' / 'blart': (colloquial) soft/cry	3. What language techniques can you identify? The accent is personified through suggestions of its strength and wiliness. Collective pronoun 'we'.	
	Lines from 'Homing': **'We heard it escape sometimes,** **a guttural *uh* on the phone to your sister,** ***saft* or *blart* to a taxi driver'**		4. What structural techniques are there? Enjambment → echoes escape of accent
6. What alternative view to this reader response might there be? Perhaps the speaker does not like the accent, as it only 'escapes' at times of relaxation (talking to sister, in a taxi).		5. How might a reader respond? The speaker seems to relish the idea of the accent escaping, like the true identity is being exposed.	

Figure 4.6: Example quotation explosion

Explore: Examining different viewpoints

Once students have got to grips with making inferences about a text, you can move on to the next stage of the schema – 'Explore'. This means examining the text in greater depth, for example by studying a specific critical viewpoint and allowing students time to assess whether they agree or disagree. In this way, students will learn to be critical about the texts they read, both fiction and non-fiction. To help develop critical skills in students, it's important to understand the process of reading and how students develop as readers.

Appleyard (1991) outlined several stages of reading:

Player: Stories are mostly play, and students place themselves within them.	**Hero:** The student empathises with characters and feels strongly about them, not fully realising they are fictional constructs.	**Thinker:** The student understands that the characters are constructs – they can comment on the author's craft and the effect on the reader.	**Interpreter:** The student begins to reason about the text and to explore different stances; they may start to explore literary criticism.	**Pragmatist:** An adult reader who has experience of many texts and decides which ones to read for information, enjoyment, etc.

Figure 4.7: Becoming a reader (adapted from Appleyard, 1991)

By secondary level, students are in the 'thinker' and 'interpreter' stages of reading. They understand characters as constructs and the ways that a writer crafts language, but they can also explore different ideas about a text through reasoning and start to analyse and evaluate different interpretations. This is the point at which we need to fully activate students' critical-thinking skills, to help them remember details and, ultimately, to make judgements about a text.

In 2021, the AQA GCSE English Literature paper asked students to explore the character of the female protagonist with the following question:

> *Act II Scene i. Starting with this conversation, explore how far Shakespeare presents Juliet as a female character with strong emotions.*
>
> *Write about:*
> * *how Shakespeare presents Juliet in this extract*
> * *how far Shakespeare presents Juliet as a female character with strong emotions in the play as a whole.*

The question requires students to be both a thinker and an interpreter. A good response would use a combination of different types of knowledge, as shown in the table on the next page:
* declarative knowledge (shown in bold)
* *non-declarative knowledge* about how to structure a response (shown in italics)
* literary reasoning (shown in roman).

Thinker	Interpreter
• **Knows details of Juliet's mixed feelings about Romeo and his actions.**	• Identifies the use of contrast in the attitude towards Romeo and Juliet's relationship, e.g. Juliet is 'too rash, too unadvis'd, too sudden' while to Romeo is shown to have a more impulsive/risky attitude.
• **Understands details of the strength of Juliet's love for Romeo.**	
• **Identifies details of her defiance of her parents' wishes, e.g. that she marry Paris.**	• Explores Juliet's position in society – the only daughter of a noble family with certain expectations.
• Recognises that she is capable of secrecy/deception but is realistic about her relationship.	• Includes ideas about gender – Juliet defies conventional expectations of girls at the time.
• Highlights the use of oxymoronic images to describe Romeo, e.g. 'damn'd saint', 'dove-feathered raven'.	• Explores ideas of fate versus free will.
• Identifies when Juliet is referred to as 'disobedient wretch', 'headstrong'.	• *Includes a thesis which runs through entire piece.*
• *Understands how to structure a response with evidence supporting interpretations.*	

In their report on this question (AQA, November 2021), the examiners mentioned that the best answers were focused on the task and developed an overall thesis or argument. They concluded:

> ❛ *Overall, those students who spent time thinking about the focus of the question performed better than those who provided a response just to the text rather than to the text through the lens of the task [...]. Stronger responses are frequently characterised by having an opening thesis which demonstrates an overall response to the whole text and acknowledges the general focus of the question.* ❜

In my experience, focusing on declarative knowledge will result in students being more likely to simply regurgitate answers and recount facts about a text, rather than really explore the question. As the AQA report suggests, classrooms that are focused on developing literary reasoning and building non-declarative knowledge in how to structure a response are more likely to produce students capable of authentic responses to the text, focusing on the task.

You can encourage this approach in several ways. For example, rather than giving students a list of vocabulary and technical terms to support them in basic comprehension and identifying features of a text, use a DART technique like table completion or creating a diagram to encourage exploration of themes and ideas. The example in Figure 4.6 shows how students could match images to a text (in the form of a diagram) and consider their connotations to give an insight into Juliet's state of mind. This approach helps students to draw out a thesis that they can explore in their writing.

JULIET O serpent heart. hid with a flow'ring face!
Did ever dragon keep so fair a cave?
Beautiful tyrant. fiend angelical!
Dove-feathered raven. wolvish-ravening lamb!
Despised substance of divinest show!
Just opposite to what thou justly seem'st.
A damned saint. an honourable villain!
O nature. what hadst thou to do in hell
When thou didst bower the spirit of a fiend
In mortal paradise of such sweet flesh?
Was ever book containing such vile matter
So fairly bound? O that deceit should dwell
In such a gorgeous palace!

Can you pair up these images?

What links them?

Why do you think Juliet uses them now?

What could we say about her state of mind?

Figure 4.8: An approach to exploring Shakespeare

Students may note that Juliet is lamenting the death of her cousin and questioning Romeo's character. They may recognise that the raven and the deathly figure in the images highlight the sombre tone of the text. They can also see a dove as a representation of abstract love, and with the help of teacher questioning they may conclude that Juliet is somewhat conflicted here. They may make links with the animals and suggest that Juliet uses animalistic imagery here to acknowledge basic human needs and desires.

Through questioning (*What is...? Where is...? Why might...? How does...?*), you could then zoom in on the repeated use of oxymoron in, for instance, 'dove-feathered raven'. Students may continue to think about this conflict and, based on her repetition of the idea that Romeo's outside beauty (the dove) conceals a monster within (the raven), they may come up with the thesis that Juliet is indecisive in her feelings towards Romeo. The nature of this questioning encourages literary reasoning, linking individual features of the words to an overall idea that expresses an understanding of Juliet's state of mind.

Drama for reading

To explore a text fully, students ideally need to experience the drama of the piece. In 2018, I was able to take a group of students in the Middle East to a memorable performance in the desert of the National Theatre's production of *Frankenstein*, starring Jonny Lee Miller and Benedict Cumberbatch. The experience transformed students' understanding of the horrors of the story and allowed them to produce insightful and developed exam answers for GCSE. We were also visited by an actress from Shakespeare's Globe in 2017, who performed an immersive performance of *Romeo and Juliet*. Year 7 students were called on to be Mercutio and the Nurse – an experience that engaged them in the characters' motivations and feelings throughout the play. It was a joy to watch, and the English department was able to weave the benefits of this immersion into the scheme of work.

Not everyone will have access to external sources like this to bring the drama of literature to life, but it is still possible to use dramatic techniques in your teaching. Here are some suggestions:

Improvisation	Students form a circle. One student starts by improvising what a character might do. Mr Birling might be welcoming the Inspector, for instance, showing disdain and superiority. The next student in the circle asks: 'What are you doing?' The student tells them something else (Sheila complaining about Eva Smith) and the new student has to improvise this new action. You can come up with the new actions yourself if your students might find this difficult.
The given circumstances	Explore what students know about a text and challenge assumptions they might make. You can consider the given circumstances by asking questions such as: Where are we? Who are we? Why are we? Students may assume that a character with the name 'Sandy' is female, so it is useful to explore how this could be incorrect.
Conscience alley	Students create an 'alley' by standing in two lines. Another student, as a 'character', walks down the alley while the students on either side call out comments about the character's actions from the viewpoint of other characters within the text. This allows exploration of the validity of thoughts and ideas of characters in the play or book. When the character reaches the end of the alley, the student should reflect on what they heard and decide, through discussion, whether this alters their view of the character.
Flashback/ flashforward	Critically explore the situations of different characters at certain points of the play. Consider Juliet and her position at the play's start then flash forward to where she is being forced to marry Paris, her connection with Romeo and how these change our perception of her as a character.
Thought-tracking	Speak aloud the thought process of characters to break down motivations for students. You might take the moment Juliet decides to marry Romeo and how she comes to the conclusion that her love for him overrides her other responsibilities. Model this first and then allow them to have a go. Students could do the same for Romeo and then explore if the characters' aims and motivations differ.

You can bring drama to your English Literature and Language classes without the hassle of booking the drama studio or even moving desks. For example:

- Hot-seat a character from *An Inspector Calls* at a particular moment in the play to explore their motivations and make predictions for the rest of the play.
- Put students in small groups and ask them to create a freeze-frame of the action in Simon Armitage's poem 'Remains' to explore the imagery and the impact this might have on a reader.
- Make half the room a modern audience and half the room a Shakespearean audience, and consider their different responses to a key scene in *Macbeth* to explore a feminist reading of Lady Macbeth.
- Ask groups of students to put together some theatrical reproductions of real-life events to be discussed by the class in preparation for writing non-fiction texts.

Drama can also help students to develop the skills required to respond to a text and its meaning. The principles of drama can be used to help students develop skills in exploring characters' feelings and motivations and to build a thesis about the impact of dramatic representation. The first question an actor may ask is 'What is my objective?', so encouraging students to reflect on this when considering characters will really help them to focus on ideas and intent. For example, asking '*What is Romeo's objective in this scene?*' allows students to condense their understanding of the action in a scene into a single objective for the character which can then support a written analysis.

This can be further developed to explore tactics – investigating how a character achieves their objective. Re-enacting parts of the drama and trying out different objectives for the same character can really support students in deciding what the character's true intent is in the scene. It can also shed light on any ambiguities in the way the character and their intentions have been portrayed and the different interpretations that may result.

Finally, the dramatic technique of 'beats' can help students to gain a sense of the overall meaning of a text. Beats are emotions or intentions that can be attributed to a line of text, encapsulating the action moment by moment. They are essentially instructions for how the line could be delivered. For example, you could apply the following beats to these lines from Othello's speech in Act I Scene 3:

Line	Beat
Most potent, grave, and reverend signiors,	Respect
My very noble and approved good masters: That I	Flatter
have ta'en away this old man's daughter, It is	Contest
most true; true I have married her.	Admit to

The beats are, of course, open to interpretation, so choosing beats offers students a great opportunity to explore ambiguity in a text. It also allows them to summarise their understanding of a character's feelings, intentions, tone or motivations, to bring greater insight. Remember, you can use low-stakes interaction with drama if performance might overwhelm your students, but generally the more drama in the classroom, the better!

Exploring poetry

Sharing poetry and exploring its meaning with the class is a great way to practise skills of inference and understanding abstract meaning. However, bringing too much structure to the study of poetry can be a detriment to the experience; a loose structure with the opportunity for students to provide authentic responses is best. Start by listening to the poem being read aloud and allow students to feel the rhythm and music of the lines. Sharing lyrics is a useful way to show students how poetry is like song.

Consider the poem 'Home' by Warsan Shire, who has also written lyrics for Beyoncé. (You can find the poem in Shire's book *Bless the Daughter Raised by a Voice in her Head*.) The contemporary topic and combination of language devices make this an engaging choice to share with your students, though be aware that the content may not be appropriate for all students so will need sensitive handling (there is reference to sexual assault).

You could explore the opening stanzas as shown in Figure 4.9.

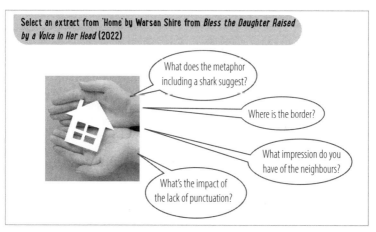

Figure 4.9: Exploring 'Home' by Warsan Shire

Shire uses repetition of 'home' throughout the poem to represent love but also danger. The tragedy of home being unsafe resonates with the reader as it is likely to be something they are aware of (or have perhaps even experienced themselves). Metaphors and symbolism are used cleverly (the mouth of a shark and the barrel of a gun as images for home). The symbolism of home distils the despair and fear that permeates the whole poem.

In exploring and making judgements about poetry, you might like to follow a process like this:

- **Feel:** What does the poem make you feel? What do you notice about the rhythm? Which words resonate with you? Which sounds?
- **Listen:** Who is speaking? What is the voice of the poem? What might they be trying to say?
- **Explore meaning:** What does the poem literally mean? Are there any metaphors or other language devices that add different layers of meaning?
- **Look at structure:** What is the shape of the poem? Where is the punctuation? Where do I breathe? How many stanzas are there? Does this add to meaning?
- **Consider clarity:** Is anything unclear? Is there any ambiguity we might explore here?

Reflection

- What drama texts have you used recently in your teaching of reading?
- What opportunities for drama activities could you incorporate into your reading lessons this week?
- How might using a 'dramatic' approach support your students' understanding of the motivations, emotions and intentions of characters in a text you are reading?
- How easy do you think it will be to get your students to perform? How comfortable do you feel modelling performance for the class?
- Are there any opportunities for your class to see drama in action? (You could check with your head of department if actors could come to your school.)
- How might you develop your reading of poetry?

Judge: Interpreting and evaluating texts

The final stage in the schema involves interpreting a text and making judgements about it. In order to do this, students need to consider one more key character – the writer themselves. This means making inferences about the writer's intentions and how they may have wanted the reader to feel at particular points in a text. I find it useful to give students a loose structure for exploring these aspects of a text and then applying their ideas in analytical writing:

thought → example → intent

A *thought* is an idea about the text. For example, in Kit de Waal's novel *My Name is Leon*, the reader feels intense sympathy for Leon when he is separated from his little brother, Jake. An *example* of this is when de Waal writes: 'the baby is like a television. Leon can't stop watching him and all his baby movements.' This suggests that Leon is captivated by Jake. The writer's *intention* is to show the injustice and racism in society and how that negatively impacts these brothers' lives when Jake is adopted but Leon isn't.

Giving students verb stems (for example, 'The writer *fears/adores/rejects/hopes...*') will help them to structure their responses clearly. So, here the judgement might be that de Waal rejects the underlying injustice and racism in the system that separates the two brothers.

Task

Choose a text you will be using with your students this week. Note down some thoughts and feelings in a table like the one below that will support your students to decipher the writer's intent.

Thought	Example	Intent
		fears
		adores
		rejects
		hopes

Structuring written responses

When students make evaluations about the text, they summarise their judgements in written paragraphs. Remember that this is a reading skill, even though students are expressing their evaluations about reading in writing.

Many teachers use PEE (or PEEL/PETAL) to help students structure their thoughts and eventually their paragraphs in a written response. However, AQA notes: 'While this approach does provide a structure which is helpful in learning how to approach exam responses, it is a scaffold which should be removed once the candidate is more secure' (quoted in Oliver, 2017). Students need to be developing an *overall* thesis or argument for their response, and PEE and similar structures only support students in making individual points, so while they may have some value when students begin to write analytically, you should plan to remove them as they become more confident. This way, they won't lose sight of the overall thesis and will be able to produce responses that fully explore the task using relevant evidence and strong explanations.

The PEE structure focuses on comprehension (AO1); it doesn't encourage much exploration of language and its effects so on its own it won't generate a full answer to any task. In Chapter 2 of *Curriculum with Soul*, Jo Heathcote offers a different approach to embed a broader analysis and hit all the objectives. She frames her response to exam tasks with further questions: 'The higher-tariff skills of AO3 and AO4 for English Language I presented as "The What-How Combos" where both AO1 and AO2 skills are required to be shown in a combination and developed.' Adding structured questions as scaffolding for students at each stage of the writing process encourages an inquisitive approach, allowing them to question the text in greater depth.

A useful technique for creating a coherent thesis based on connected ideas is to plot out five points and then consider what thesis might connect them by exploring key words and ideas. The following is an example of this based on *A Christmas Carol*.

Task	Explore how Dickens presents the effects of loneliness and isolation in **A Christmas Carol**.				
Points	1. Scrooge, the protagonist, is an isolated and lonely character.	2. Prominence of love and compassion.	3. Display of happy, loving families and groups: Cratchits, Fred, Fezziwig.	4. Ideas about humanity and morality.	5. Ideas about the value of charity and kindness.
Key themes/ words	Family, compassion, kindness, community, lack of isolation				
Thesis	Dickens is using the novel as a social manifesto, showing the reader what he thinks is important for a moral life.				

Once they have their thesis, encourage students to use iterations of it in each paragraph of their written response, using phrases such as: 'further explores', 'this is compounded with', 'again we see this when…'.

Live modelling

At the start of students' journey into analytical writing, it's also important to expose the thought processes behind analysis so they can replicate this. Live modelling in class is the best way of helping students to understand how to think critically and how to convey that effectively in their writing (as we explored in Chapter 2). The example below shows how you could live model the thought process involved in responding to the following question: *How is the tragedy of King Lear portrayed to the audience?*

Thesis: The unendurable sadness of the play is highlighted through Cordelia's death where the audience are left looking for answers which do not come.	
Thought process	**Written response**
First, I must ensure that I understand the question and decide how tragedy is articulated within the play. I will decide where moments of tragedy are and select the most poignant.	The tragedy of King Lear is exposed in the inexplicable hanging of his favourite daughter.
Lear's response to Cordelia's death is unbearable. I need to select a quotation that portrays this and includes language that I can analyse. The root of Lear's sadness and anger is that this death is inexplicable – I'll add that to my thesis statement. I have my judicious evidence and can give a sense of the character's feelings through my choice of verb 'laments'.	He begins to see more clearly here and laments: 'Had I your tongues and eyes, I'd use them so / That heaven's vault should crack.'
Now I am going to explore some of the connotations and draw out inferences from the quotation. (AO1)	The imagery of 'tongues' and 'eyes' suggests some insight which Lear is lacking. He cannot see and he cannot articulate what has been seen.
Now I should forensically explore the method(s) Shakespeare is using here. I need to ensure that I am focused on the question and relating my ideas to my thesis. I need to explore how the audience and/or I as reader may respond to those creative choices, again linking this to the question. (AO2)	His literal wish to break 'heaven's vault' highlights the love and esteem Lear feels for Cordelia and the onomatopoeic 'crack' escalates the idea of destruction and the tragedy of losing her. The audience wants answers to Cordelia's death – but these never come. Shakespeare uses this fact to intensify the unbearable sadness of the play.
How might the social, political, historical or literary context be relevant here? What might it show us linked to the writer's possible message or intentions? What can we infer that supports our thesis? (AO3)	This is compounded by the social order of the kingdom being disrupted as Lear splits his kingdom in two between his two remaining daughters, affecting the contemporary audience because...

The live model doesn't have to be perfect, it just needs to clearly show your approach to writing. Don't give students the model without talking through its discrete parts first. It may be useful for them to see an end product, but it would be impossible for them to replicate it without knowing the cognitive process of how it has been produced.

When students aren't constrained by feeling that they have to regurgitate knowledge about texts and/or reproduce structures that can be limiting, they can respond well and imaginatively to what they read, as is often noted in AQA's GCSE English Literature examiner's reports, in relation to the unseen poetry question.

Exploring success criteria

Having said that, students still need to understand what makes a paragraph successful. Once again, there are alternative ways to approach this rather than following PEE-type structures. Choosing instead to reinforce success criteria for a task allows students to include their analysis, methods and evidence in any order that seems clear and logical to them, and also gives them a good framework for peer assessment.

The examiner says...	The teacher says...	The student says...
Critical, exploratory response.	Thesis?	The theme of X is exposed to be...
Judicious use of precise references to support interpretation(s).	Alternative view?	It could be seen to be... Potentially... An alternative interpretation...
Analysis of writer's methods with subject terminology used judiciously.	Evidence? Methods?	This is suggested in... This is exposed through...
Exploration of effects of writer's methods to create meanings.	Connotations? Response?	Imagery/personification/oxymoron... X suggests... X escalates...
Exploration of ideas/perspectives/contextual factors shown by specific, detailed links between context/text/task.	Perspective?	The reader may sense... The audience feels... A modern audience may respond... The contemporary reader would surmise...

Task

Think about an extract you might read with your class this week. Note down a model response to a question, based on success criteria that you will narrate for the class.

Question:		
Extract/quotations	**Success**	**Model response**
	Thesis?	
	Alternative view?	
	Evidence?	
	Methods?	
	Connotations?	
	Response?	
	Perspective?	

Reflection

- How have you used PEE or similar structures in your classroom? What alternative structures might you consider using now?
- How could you use the five-point plan to encourage reasoning and draw out a thesis?
- What do you need to do to prepare for live modelling?
- What are the success criteria you need to draw out?

Removing scaffolds

As your students develop the skills for producing effective written responses to reading texts, it is best to remove any scaffolds you have been using incrementally. Start with a more questioning approach, using a scaffold that encourages an inquisition of the text, then move on by removing the rigidity of the scaffold by live modelling and deconstructing model responses with the class. Collaborating on construction can also help students to understand the analytical process. Finally, allowing students to generate and use a five-point plan alongside some success criteria will encourage their creativity.

You can split this process of removing scaffolds into three phases:

Phase 1	Provide scaffolds with leading questions (e.g. 'What is the effect of the language technique?')
	Provide models, highlighted in line with success criteria.
	Give students sentence starters (e.g. 'The personification in . . .').
Phase 2	Live model and articulate your thought process.
	Give students a scaffold with thought prompts.
	Collaborate to create model responses and then deconstruct these.
	Give students key verbs and phrases to use in their response (e.g. 'connotes', 'further implies').
Phase 3	Use a five-point plan and give students success criteria to refer to.
	Look at whole responses and explore how points interconnect.

Scaffolding the reading of complex texts

To scaffold the reading of complex texts (particularly those from the nineteenth century and Shakespeare) and to assist students in effective evaluation, make sure you explain literal meanings, explore glossaries and images, identify grammatical structures, teach common whole-text structures (e.g. What makes this Gothic? Why is this tragic?) and features of specific forms or genres, and help students to explore the abstract and figurative meanings of words. All these strategies target the teaching of complex texts by scaffolding the experience for the reader. Ask yourself:

- Could I break down the complexity by teaching the text using extracts?
- Could I embed glossaries or scaffolded questions for students?
- Where could I isolate and teach figurative language using tenor, vehicle and ground?
- Have I explained the text's specific genre or form and structure?

Rethinking context

Context is the situation out of which the text arises and is responsive to the situation in which it is read (which may vary between students) – that is, it's about how the text is currently or has been received, and different readers' responses at different times. In being assessed for their understanding of context (AO3), students are expected to 'show understanding of the relationships between texts and the contexts in which they were written'. This refers to time/historical context, of course, but it also refers to genre. There is a lot of focus on the historical context in schools, but literary context is also relevant to this assessment objective, so having a clear knowledge of the conventions of genre can really support students in successfully meeting this criterium.

Since 2015, most exam boards have encouraged schools to take a text-led and holistic approach to understanding context, and your students will have myriad responses to the texts they read for their English lessons. I once taught John Agard's poem 'Checking Out Me History' to a class in Dubai. Because of their varied heritages, many students weren't familiar with the story behind Agard's imagery of the dish running away with the spoon. However, they could see straight away that this was nursery/nonsense rhyme, and this understanding gave them a critical insight into the poem despite the fact that their own heritage of nursery rhymes differed from that in the UK.

Responses will be personal, and it's important to ensure that they are heard and valued, even if they are drawn from reference points, such as social media, that you might not be personally acquainted with. Authentic responses are key to AO3 and enable students to move away from an exclusive focus on historical context, which shows knowledge but does not necessarily provide a critical insight into the text or task.

Deconstructing model judgements

In order for students to make confident judgements in their responses to reading texts, make sure you explore the ingredients of a successful response with your students. For example, a GCSE English Language paper question may be: 'Compare how the writers convey their different thoughts and feelings about experiences of cycling.' To explore what would make a successful response to this, start by working through some success criteria in the form of questions to get students thinking:

- What methods are used here?
- How are the different methods used?
- What evidence from both texts supports this?
- What are the different ideas and perspectives in both texts?

At this point, it is useful for students to predict what they might expect to see in the model response. For example, they might be able to tell you which methods they would expect to see or the phrasing normally used to explore perspective. When deconstructing responses, it helps to begin by modelling for students how to identify specific success criteria in the model response by selecting a different colour or style for each question and highlighting where success is evident. Later, students should be able to do this for themselves. One example is shown on the next page.

In the first text, the writer asserts that she remembers cycling on holiday with *'trepidation and anxiety'*, which suggests that her first experiences were not positive. The noun *'trepidation'* implies fear and dread. In contrast, the second writer discusses racing on his bike with positive imagery: *'I crossed the finish line and my heart, beating so fast throughout the race, burst into a thousand pieces.'* The image of the heart bursting escalates the happiness he felt as he won the race.	Where are methods identified? *What evidence is used?* Are differences explored?

Ultimately, reading is the foundation of everything we do in English and the starting point should be a varied diet of engaging texts for students to enjoy. Embedding texts that celebrate diversity is vital here, to allow all students to find a point of connection with what they are reading, and to counteract the issue that recent research from Newcastle University identifies: 'that [teachers may] have been *taught* to see racial diversity as a problem' (Smith and Lander, 2023). Then, by following the schema for reading outlined in this chapter, you will give students the tools to become expert and engaged readers, connecting with texts, and inferring and interpreting with pleasure, both in the classroom and for life.

Strategies and takeaways

- **Read for pleasure:** Following the schema for reading can enhance reading skills, making it more likely students will read for pleasure, which has a huge impact on their attainment and enjoyment.
- **Just read:** A fast-paced, immersive read of the text can support readers of all levels, stopping for more complex parts and using the schema to support this.
- **Diminish difficulty:** Use strategies to support reading of complex texts; quotation explosions and responsive reading can support more analytical responses.
- **Model it:** Live modelling and exposing the thought process is more effective than PEE structures. Use these scaffolds, but remember to gradually remove them.
- **Play with the words:** Actively engaging with drama can bring your classroom alive.

Chapter 5: The craft of writing

Simply put, writing is a means of expressing feelings and thoughts on paper. This is a personal process, and you should encourage your students to write in a free and artful manner, demonstrating their creativity. Unlike speech, which is ephemeral, writing is permanent and can be regarded as a record of other artistic forms, such as speech, ideas or songs. It is essential that we, as teachers, take this as our starting point. Accuracy of expression can be developed and honed once students have been empowered to create their stories, lines of argument and conceptual theses themselves.

Start with feelings, not form or features

In an attempt to support students, there has long been an overemphasis on form, structure and features rather than feelings and ideas. However, taking a 'feelings and ideas first' approach will add believability and authenticity to students' writing, avoiding mechanical, constructed pieces. I recently observed a lesson by a conscientious trainee teacher who asked students to write a fictional piece built around the idea of jealousy, beginning with a description of the weather using pathetic fallacy. Many students struggled because the teacher had not explained what jealousy was and the class had not explored useful ideas such as how jealousy might manifest in a person or what it meant to young people. They diligently used the feature of pathetic fallacy, but it had no relevance to feelings of envy or resentment. When responses lack authenticity in this way, readers will not be engaged in the piece, and students will not experience the enjoyment of writing, which should be free and creative rather than mechanical.

Another example of how form is often emphasised over feeling is the use of PEE paragraphs in critical writing. As discussed in Chapter 4, modelling how we articulate thought processes in analytical as well as creative and non-fiction writing is key to helping students structure their own responses. They should write like readers, always keeping in mind the pleasure that comes from reading well-crafted pieces as they hone their own writing skills.

One way of encouraging authenticity in writing is to follow a sequence from reading into writing (Rose, 2016). Below is an example of a sequence that I have adapted to develop reading (bold) into writing (roman) through talk (*italic*).

Text scale	Strategies
Whole text	**Literal reading**
Short passages	**Inferential reading**
Sentences	*Interpretative talk activities*
Short passages	Collaborative rewriting
Whole texts	Joint construction
Metacognition	*Review of what has been learnt*

GCSE examiners are crying out for students to write authentically, as this recent AQA report reveals:

> ❝Students could be reminded that the image is a prompt for their own, related ideas and they can offer ideas from their own imagination to provide more control over the direction of their writing. Some students had leant heavily upon "learned" responses, the details of which are quickly recognisable and do not often add to their piece.❞
> AQA GCSE English Language Paper 1, Examiner Report (2021)

Teachers are under a lot of pressure to achieve results. As a Head of English, I was pressured into using a restrictive strategy because senior leadership was enforcing a prescribed approach to persuasive writing:

- Line 1: Use a one-sentence paragraph.
- Line 2: Include a semicolon.
- Line 3: Add a rhetorical question, etc.

It is also often assumed that cognitive processes that work in other subjects can be applied to English. For example, the process of using declarative knowledge when writing about organisms in science using a structure dictated by the acronym MRS GREN (Movement, Respiration, Sensitivity, Growth, Reproduction, Excretion, Nutrition) is often translated into an English context in persuasive writing using the acronym AFOREST (Alliteration, Facts, Opinion, Rhetorical questions, Emotive language, Statistics, Triples). The cognitive process works in science, where students are not required to develop a believable 'voice'. However, in English it encourages them to use a fixed number of linguistic devices at the expense of planning inspiring content focused on their own ideas, views and feelings and connecting to the reader. Students should be prompted to ask questions in English, not to remember declarative facts.

Pedagogical schema for writing

It can be useful to approach the process of writing – from initial ideas to a developed draft – using a schema like the one below.

Writing	Spark	Define	Draft	Compare	Refine	Develop
	Set the focus for writing; elicit ideas.	*Identify the audience; explore genre and text type.*	*Use scaffolds to support the initial writing phase.*	*Live model and compare to sentence-level examples.*	*Consider live modelling; revisit success*	*Ask students to redraft after reflection; use metacognitive strategies.*

Spark: Setting the focus for writing

Any process leading to writing needs to include an ideas stage. Remember, the ability to ignite ideas from students' own imagination and to think creatively are skills that are useful beyond the classroom, and many employers value these abilities. There is also a strong argument that encouraging independent expression through writing can contribute to mental wellbeing.

Using talk

Talk is a great way to generate individual pieces. Consider the following step-by-step approach to using talk as the first stage in creating a piece of persuasive writing.

Step 1

Firstly, set a focus for writing, such as how the internet or social media has changed the way humans communicate. You want to encourage authentic ideas – something personal and believable. Start with some questions that students can think about independently, such as:

- What is communication?
- What makes it valuable?
- How do you communicate best?
- How might your communication be improved?
- What is social media?
- What does it mean to you?
- What is one example of when you use social media?

Now, spark some ideas. Get students on their feet and ask them where they stand on an issue, such as the proposition: 'Social media has improved human communication.' The first time they consider this issue, they should vote 'with their feet' – moving to one side of the room depending on whether they agree or disagree with the statement. They can stand in the middle of the room if they are unsure. They should do this first part of the activity in silence, considering the issue and making a decision on their own.

Next, ask students to pair up with someone on the opposite side of the room and to discuss why they hold opposing views. They should use concrete examples – either facts they know or evidence from a text they may have studied – to explain their point of view. After this discussion, ask students if their opinion has changed and allow them to move to a different part of the room if they want to. If they are undecided, they can stay where they are and listen to ideas from those with firmer views later on.

Finally, share ideas as a whole class. Cold call some students and ask them to explain their viewpoint and to give one example of why they think this. You could collate ideas on the board and model ways of expressing them well, collecting vocabulary to use in scaffolding later.

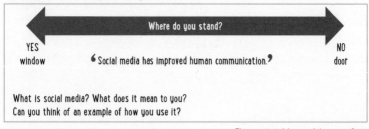

Figure 5.1: Vote with your feet

Step 2

Ask students to return to their seats and to use a mini whiteboard to practise expressing in writing some of the ideas they have talked about. They can summarise their ideas with an 'I believe...' statement and hold these up for you and the rest of the class to see. If you think it would be helpful, provide students with some vocabulary to support their expression – for example, for this topic you might suggest the words 'interaction', 'wellbeing', 'relationship', 'immediacy' and 'detrimental' to help generate some well-phrased ideas.

Step 3

Now it's time for students to consider both sides of the argument. Collate the views for and against the statement in a table on the board. Through questioning, encourage students to think about what is missing. Have we explored all aspects of communication? All the impacts of a lack of face-to-face communication? Every stakeholder involved? They can explore this with a partner and build their personal responses, then share any new ideas through a dialogic discussion with the entire class.

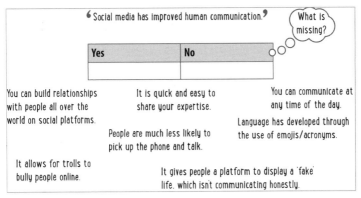

Figure 5.2: Building an argument

Step 4

Next, introduce some ideas about structure and accuracy, explaining that these are guidelines that students can use to give their writing some direction. For instance, you could suggest that they start their piece with an argument in favour of their opinion in the motion, make use of comparative connectives to structure ideas ('initially', 'in contrast with', 'however', etc.). They might like to deviate from the norm of the genre as they become more confident writers.

You will notice that this initial process focuses on ideas rather than techniques. Techniques are useful, but only after students have come up with some of their own ideas and developed some personal responses to a task. Doing it this way round encourages originality and adds interest to students' writing, helping them to avoid formulaic responses.

The steps above use the example of a piece of persuasive writing, but you can follow a similar process to spark ideas for other forms of writing. For a piece of creative writing, for example, you could zoom in on a visual stimulus to create an idea, such as 'I believe the woman in the picture feels lonely'. For a literature response, you might suggest the view that by the end of *A Christmas Carol*, Scrooge is absolved of all his sins. The exploration of initial ideas can then follow the same steps.

Reflection

- When have you used acronyms such as AFOREST to support students' writing and what kind of responses have they generated?

- How do you feel about teaching writing with a focus on ideas and feelings first?

- What opportunities might there be if you adopted this approach in your classroom? What, if any, limitations can you identify?

Task

Think about a writing task in which students need to explore two points of view. Using a table like the one below, create a plan for a discussion prior to writing.

Statement to debate:	
Vote with your feet	Decide on a stance and then work in pairs to justify your point of view.
	Try to convince someone on the other side of the room of your point of view. Why have you stood here? What concrete examples can you give?
Cold call as a class	Did you change your position? If so, why? What is the impact of your evidence on your partner's opinion of the motion?
Mini-whiteboard response	Words to support:
Table task	Ideas summarised:
Structure for writing	Persuasive speech; analytical response.

Free writing

It is important not to introduce a model too early in the writing schema, otherwise students may be tempted simply to mimic the model rather than applying their own creativity to the task. Modelling also shifts the focus away from ideas, thoughts and feelings towards form. Instead, in the 'Spark' stage of the schema, encourage students to enjoy some free writing. Elbow (1995) defines this as a process of just writing, rather than being concerned about accuracy or success criteria, and states that practising free-writing can have a powerful effect on *all* writing output. In part, this is because compulsive, premature editing makes writing difficult and dampens the 'voice'. Free writing – in which no editing takes place – allows the writer's voice to surface, as they start to articulate what they think, and makes the writing process more enjoyable.

It is helpful to allow time for free writing once the broad aims for writing have been established, but before you rigidly define success criteria. To encourage innovation in students, try not to constrain them by prescribing what success looks like too early in the process. It is good to devote some time to writing weekly – perhaps your last lesson of the week.

One way to ignite creativity is to access the English and Media Centre's 'Just Write' programme, which contains activities to inspire students to write with freedom and creativity across fiction, non-fiction and poetry.

> **Reflection**
> - Can you imagine giving students a short free-writing task? What are the limitations?
> - Could you give students a short free-writing task this week and reflect on the impact on their writing?

Define: Identifying text type and audience

For the next part of the schema, you need to establish the type of text students will be writing. Research by Rose and Martin (2012) and Gibbons (2015) into a sequence for writing explores how specific teaching strategies can provide students with useful frameworks for different genres of writing. These strategies include investigating the goal for the piece before looking at models and then refining the aims.

Defining the aims of a piece of writing requires an understanding of audience – who is this piece of writing *for*? Sometimes the audience is stated explicitly in a task, for example, 'Write an email to your headteacher giving your opinion on school uniform'. But in others, particularly in creative writing tasks, the audience can be harder to discern, for example in a task such as 'Write about a joyful moment'.

The first step is to define the text's purpose so that students know the right features to include to engage their audience. Halliday and Martin (1993) define six key text types:

- Instruction
- Recount
- Explanation
- Information
- Persuasion
- Discussion.

This has formed the basis of the National Literacy Strategy's approach to texts, emphasising the role that purpose and audience have in dictating form. To support your students, encourage them to ask the following questions:

- Overall purpose: What is my purpose (what text type am I producing)? Am I entertaining, persuading or informing readers?
- Standpoint: Who might be interested in this piece? What am I trying to convey to the reader? What is my view on the topic? What tone will my writing take?
- Audience: So, who might my intended audience be? A single individual? A group of people? The general public?

Corbett and Strong (2021) suggest that exploring the typical structural features (such as topic sentences and chronological events) and typical language features (for example, emotive language or comparative connectives) of each text type allows writers to think about how best to engage the audience. So, before students start writing it is essential to ensure they know the answers to these questions:

- What is the text type? (purpose)
- What is my standpoint on the topic? (for example, I agree with the motion)
- Who is the audience?
- What language works best?
- What structure will work best?

The following table outlines some guidance for each text type, including appropriate language and possible structures.

Text type	Purpose	Language
Instruction	To direct or tell	Imperative verbs Formal, impersonal tone
Recount	To narrate or describe	Time connectives Imagery
Explanation	To delineate or express	Short, simple sentences Impersonal tone
Information	To advise or inform	Time connectives Impersonal tone
Persuasion	To convince or persuade	Opinion Rhetoric Personal tone
Discussion	To debate or explore	Evidence Comparative connectives

How might this work in practice for the motion we looked at earlier? Look at this task:

> Convince readers of your school magazine that social media has improved communication.

We can dialogically define our aims in response to the first three questions:

• What is the text type? A persuasive piece.

• What is my standpoint on the topic? Social media has improved communication.

• Who is the audience? Readers of the school magazine – students, the school community, perhaps parents.

As the purpose is to persuade an audience of a particular point of view, we can see from the table that the writing should give an opinion, take a personal tone and use rhetorical techniques.

You could use a table like the one below to structure the planning stage, thinking about what might appeal to the audience you have identified.

Text type?	Audience?	Standpoint	What appeals?	Purpose?
Persuasion	Readers of the school magazine	Social media is a good thing, improving communication	References to the school community Ideas about the impact on education Direct address – engaging them in the text	Convince/persuade

Draft: Scaffolding writing

While it is important to make time in the classroom for independent free writing, of course you also need to integrate the more pragmatic elements of the writing schema, to help students develop the skills they need to write for purpose and effect. There will be more time for independent learning in the final stage of the schema, where students redraft their writing.

Begin the 'Draft' stage with a scaffold to support students. You can draw on what you have decided in the 'Define' stage when zooming in on the ideas of what might appeal to a particular audience. Some students may also find it useful to have starter sentences to get them going; integrating interesting vocabulary into these starters can really support students in the process of structuring engaging ideas.

A scaffold for the task above may look like this:

Task: Convince readers of your school magazine that social media has improved communication.		
Persuade Appeal to the school community Focus on the impact on education	Starter sentences: • Firstly, it is imperative for human connection that… • Additionally, evidence states… • It could, however, be argued… • Social media could be seen to be…	Key words and phrases from the discussion: • detrimental • connection • influence • educational

Figure 5.3: Scaffold using starter sentences

As students become increasingly confident in their writing, you can take away the starter sentences and replace them with prompts for each section of the piece. Start by asking students to draft 100 words and then add to this incrementally, using peer assessment to give insightful feedback. Students can swap notebooks and reflect on the text type their partner has chosen and what they have done to appeal to the audience, asking a question about their piece in a different colour pen.

To encourage the idea of drafting and re-drafting, it is beneficial to have writing tasks spanning weeks with your classes. Non-fiction and fictional pieces can be improved with peer and teacher feedback over a number of lessons, if you keep extended writing to the last lesson of the week and improve the piece incrementally.

The scaffolds teachers use are often fixed and permanent but bear in mind that while scaffolds can inspire students to write engagingly, they may also stifle creativity and overwhelm students as they decide what to write. We will look later at how to remove scaffolded support at the right time to allow students to finalise their writing independently.

I consider analytical writing (i.e. writing about the prepared and unseen texts in the GCSE Literature and Language exams) as a reading skill (see Chapter 4), so will focus here on creative and non-fiction writing.

Non-fiction scaffold

As exemplified above, when approaching non-fiction writing explore ideas and responses first and then establish clear aims in the 'Define' and 'Refine' stages of the schema. Begin with a short initial draft – a few ideas formed in sentences – and then introduce a scaffold to help students to develop this draft.

Figure 5.3 is an example of a scaffold using starter sentences. Figure 5.4 over the page shows the next stage of a scaffold, using prompts for each paragraph. This time, the motion is: 'This house believes that AI will damage the creative industries.'

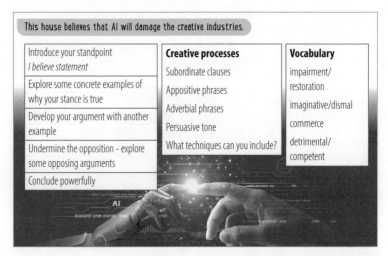

Figure 5.4: Non-fiction writing scaffold using paragraph prompts

To continue to support students, model the process using the thought-tracking drama technique from Chapter 4. Giving students vocabulary in antonym pairs will allow them to explore the alternative view and use these new words in other writing and reading tasks.

As students become more confident in writing non-fiction pieces, understanding the text type and purpose, you can gradually remove the paragraph prompts. Students can decide on their own structure for the piece, allowing them to be inventive and more creative in how they present their arguments.

Creative scaffold

When it comes to creative writing, give students a rough word count – such as a 100-word draft – to encourage them to think in terms of overall length rather than how many paragraphs they should write. This will leave them free to use one-word or one-line paragraphs for effect, as well as longer paragraphs, and to manipulate their language accordingly.

It's nice to give students a stimulus for their creative writing, such as an extract from literature, poetry or even an image. You can also guide them at first by suggesting some ideas for each paragraph and some engaging vocabulary. Remove this support incrementally (start by losing the sentence starters, then the vocabulary) as students become more confident writers and internalise the elements needed to structure a piece.

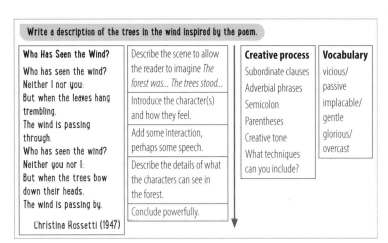

Write a description of the trees in the wind inspired by the poem.

Who Has Seen the Wind?		Creative process	Vocabulary
Who has seen the wind? Neither I nor you: But when the leaves hang trembling. The wind is passing through. Who has seen the wind? Neither you nor I: But when the trees bow down their heads. The wind is passing by. Christina Rossetti (1947)	Describe the scene to allow the reader to imagine *The forest was... The trees stood...* Introduce the character(s) and how they feel. Add some interaction, perhaps some speech. Describe the details of what the characters can see in the forest. Conclude powerfully.	Subordinate clauses Adverbial phrases Semicolon Parentheses Creative tone What techniques can you include?	vicious/ passive implacable/ gentle glorious/ overcast

Figure 5.5: Scaffold for a 100-word draft

You can also encourage creativity using music or a soundscape in the background to establish a relaxed and inspiring atmosphere in the classroom. Try some soft Mozart or the sounds of gentle rain playing (there is plenty available online) to help students focus on the creative process.

> **Reflection**
> - How have you used scaffolds when teaching writing? How effective have they been?
> - Are your scaffolds fixed and permanent, or do you already remove them gradually to encourage independent writing?
> - How might you incorporate or adapt your use of scaffolds in the classroom?

Compare: Modelling a response effectively

The next stage of the schema is to help students 'see success' through model responses. Although they should have time to write authentically before seeing how another writer has created a particular text type (especially with creative writing), it is valuable to introduce models for comparison and deconstruction after they have completed their initial drafts. Seeing sentence-level models will help students to understand effective construction and to see grammar in context. Modelling longer paragraphs will enable them to identify effective structural techniques.

Live modelling

It is a good idea to model the thought process of writing for your students, but this might be more challenging than you think! Our thoughts are so ingrained in our own schemas for writing that it can take a while to tease them out and formulate them into a clear process that can be explained to students. In fact, this is exactly what we want for students – for the cognitive process of drafting to be ingrained into their long-term memory, so that it feels automatic. How does that happen? By practising writing regularly!

So, what thoughts can we articulate for students when live modelling?

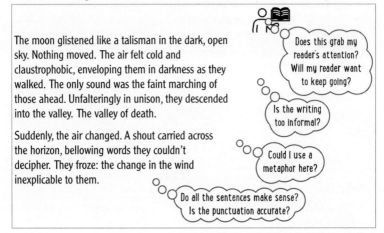

Figure 5.6: Metacognitive modelling

Try writing the extract of creative text in Figure 5.6 live with your students, using a visualiser or the board. Pause and articulate the thought process at each stage. You can even get students to feed in suggestions in a co-writing space. Make live changes as you consider the effect of certain words or lines, and always remember that your piece does not have to be perfect. Seeing you being critical of your own attempts and transforming them before their eyes will demonstrate to students how writing is a craft that can be constantly honed.

Students can then compare the model response with their own initial draft. What does the model do differently? Is it better? If so, why is it better? What does the model include that students have left out? Questioning like this can lead you to establish more developed success criteria with the class.

It can sometimes be useful to demonstrate bad models with students. When they know the text type well, they will be able to identify where the model has fallen short and suggest improvements.

Deconstructing models

Live modelling is really useful to develop students' understanding of the text type and success criteria for the task. It is equally useful to unpick and explore a completed model with students. Imagine you are teaching a creative piece. You could use the opening two paragraphs of Daphne du Maurier's novel *Rebecca* to model a piece of creative writing, then break it down with students.

Read the creative model (the extract) together and ask students to identify key language or structural features that have an impact on them as a reader:

- How is a sense of mystery developed?
- Is there anything symbolic here?
- What is the impact of the dynamic verbs?
- What is personified?
- What is the effect?

Students can compare their own creative writing to the extract using an evaluative teacher reader mode (see the 'Refine' section on pages 113 to 116).

They should look for specific things on each read. At first, they can read for an authentic response – what do they like/dislike about the piece? Then they can read for rhythm and structure (you may identify the length of the sentences as well as the immediacy created by use of the first-person voice). On a third read, focus on language, highlighting the use of personification for instance. Students can then compare to their own pieces. Have they used personification? Is their piece in the first person? Could they make changes to mimic some of the features of the model that have the kind of impact they would like to achieve themselves?

It is useful to annotate models using different coloured highlighters for different features. You can then lead an exploratory discussion about the impact of these features using planned questioning.

> **Reflection**
> - What strategies best support the development of the craft of writing?
> - How might modelling help students to write better?
> - What are the limitations of modelling in creative writing?

The meaning of words

During the processes of drafting and comparing those drafts to models, the development of writing should first be supported at word level and then at sentence level.

At word level, start with what students already know. Beck (2013) suggests introducing target words with an example of how they might be used in the context of a story, and then a student friendly explanation of meaning. If we imagine the task is to write a piece about nature, an example of Beck's process might be as follows:

Known words	Target words	Used in context	Student-friendly definition
Pecked Branch Joyous Frozen	Desolate Morosely Daintily	**Morosely, the robin pecked at the desolate, frozen earth.** Joyously, **the eager robin hopped daintily along the branch.**	Morosely means miserably or in a bad-tempered way. Desolate means without hope or encouragement. Daintily means refined and elegant.

Beck also suggests providing sentence stems that include the target words to help structure their use. For example:
- He moved daintily to...
- The desolate landscape reminded them of...

You can model this process before students begin writing their first drafts, carrying out some warm-up activities with vocabulary, sentence-level models and writing phrases. This can be consolidated after students have completed their first drafts by looking at a concrete example of the text type in the modelling stage. The sentences in the middle column can form part of the 'Compare' process during modelling (which can be whole paragraphs or sentence-level pieces). You can then break down the formulation of sentences for students as a starting point as they begin to consider how to refine and redraft their writing.

Try not to overcomplicate writing with convoluted phrasing – clarity is key. Overemphasising more complex words may undermine students' ability to express themselves accurately in their writing.

Refine: Assessing writing and responding to feedback

Reviewing drafts

Although, ultimately, students will only have 45 minutes to craft their writing in an exam, they need to understand that in most areas of life, writing is a continuous process. To help with this, it is useful to regularly model the process of drafting and redrafting work in the classroom. By providing plenty of practice in class, you will equip your students with the confidence to craft a snapshot of their best writing under exam conditions.

The process of drafting and redrafting can be demonstrated by looking at professional writers. For example, you could compare early drafts of William Blake's 'The Tyger' to the final published version.

Draft	Final
[Could fetch it from the furnace deep	What the hammer? what the chain,
And in [the *altered to*] thy horrid ribs dare steep	In what furnace was thy brain?
In the well of sanguine woe?	What the anvil? what dread grasp,
In what clay & in what mould	Dare its deadly terrors clasp!
Were thy eyes of fury roll'd? *del.*]	

Examining how Blake's final version develops the contrast of the deadly terror and the divinity of the tiger will emphasise to students the impact that careful thought and redrafting can have on their own finished pieces of writing.

Always encourage students to review their drafts, first to evaluate and then to proofread for accuracy. I like to get students to read their pieces aloud to hear how they may impact their reader and make any changes they feel are necessary at that stage. After that, go back to the success criteria you identified when comparing to models and ask how the reader might be feeling.

When reviewing, it is helpful to think about the different ways of categorising writing:

* writing as a process (planning, drafting, editing) (Hayes, 2006)
* writing a specific construction (persuasive text, analytical writing)
* writing for response (Elbow, 2000).

Eloquence in writing comes from being able to share it with different readers and gaining feedback. For each piece of work or type of writing, you should decide which 'type' of reader should give feedback.

In the classroom, it is easy to fall into the trap if just having one type of reader for students' work – you, the teacher. As such, students will only get an evaluative response. However, Elbow (2000) believes that writers do best when they have a wide audience, which encourages a variety of responses. He outlines several different 'types' of reader and the responses required to improve writing. I have adapted these in the following table:

Private reader	Peer reader	Allied reader	Teacher reader
This is the writer themselves. Students might write more honestly and fluently when they know it will not be shared. The private reader reviews their work based on model comparisons and knowledge of success criteria.	A reader of the same level who offers the writer the experience of trying to interest others.	An ally who selects the best of what someone has written and explores how to change some parts collaboratively with you.	A reader who will select the positive aspects of writing and identify areas for improvement with a specific standard in mind.
No sharing	Sharing but no response	Response but no criticism	Evaluative response

Adapted from Elbow (2000)

You do not always have to take on the role of 'teacher reader'; it's possible to support students by adopting different reader types for different tasks (or even within the same task), so they feel comfortable sharing their writing and ideas without fear of criticism and will gain the feedback needed to redraft their work effectively. Remember, too, that other students can also be 'readers'. If students are peer reviewing each other's work in this way, make sure they all have a clear understanding of the intended audience of the piece of writing in order to generate useful critical feedback. Private reading is powerful for sparking ideas.

Reflection

- How could you embed some shared writing in your lessons this week?
- What types of reader might you use to ensure students get the right feedback?

Considering feedback

Marshall and Wiliam (2006) state that the drafting phase is the most appropriate time for written feedback, but don't spend hours marking work if you don't plan for your students to respond to it. Instead, make time for response to feedback in your lessons. To ease the load of teacher marking, I would advise you make as much use as you can of peer and self-assessment. This allows for engagement from students in issues of quality and allows them to develop their own creativity. Avoid the peer and self-assessment process becoming too formulaic by structuring responses with questions:

- How do I feel as the reader?
- What is the purpose of this piece?
- Is the language engaging?
- Does the structure captivate?

Students need a clear understanding of outcome so they can participate in peer assessment. This comes through modelling. Once you have deconstructed a model with the class, define the success criteria, which can then be used in peer assessment. Students will find it much easier to critique their own or others work with this in mind. Make sure that students also understand the importance of precise praise and constructive notes when compiling feedback.

Effective redrafting

Once students have received their feedback from either you, themselves or their peers, they need to refine their writing through redrafting in line with that feedback. Encourage students to do this in a different colour pen to highlight the changes and improvements they make.

The evaluation stage can be seen as one element of 'process writing' (Hayes, 2006), which includes revision stages of reading and editing. Process writing is an approach that looks at what the writer *does*, rather than what the final piece looks like, so it is essential to activate students' thinking while they consider feedback, review and edit their work. Revisit the success criteria and features of different text types to help students evaluate the feedback they have been given (or have generated themselves as a 'private reader').

When students are self assessing, content and accuracy can be separated in the 'read' and 'edit' phases.

Content (read for feedback)	Accuracy (edit for precision)
How does this piece make me feel?	Do sentences make sense?
Are paragraphs organised by focus?	Is vocabulary used and spelt accurately?
What features are used to engage the reader?	Is my punctuation precise?
Have I used imagery to set the scene?	
Have I conveyed the feelings of the characters?	
What is the impact of longer sentences here?	

Consciously going through two stages of feedback to self-review work will ensure students keep thinking and are actively involved in the improvement of their piece. Exploring choice and effect can be seen as part of the redrafting phase, and exploring technical accuracy as editing. To keep the writing process engaging, encourage students to redraft first and then hone accuracy later on.

Develop: Finalising writing

Securing confidence in vocabulary

Scaffolds that can be gradually removed are especially useful in the 'Develop' stage of the schema. The main thing students need in their scaffold is vocabulary, and this should be taught in such a way that students can apply the thinking and language to a variety of tasks.

As well as sharing antonym pairs and exploring vocabulary that has been used in other tasks through retrieval practice, teaching the roots of words will support students in reusing words, as well as supporting them with their reading. Passages in the GCSE English Language exam papers may contain words that some students will find challenging, but understanding root words will help these students to make educated guesses about meaning. For example, knowing that 'jud' is a Latin root meaning 'judge' will help students to decipher the meaning of 'judicious' and 'prejudice', and knowing that 'rupt' comes from the Latin meaning 'to break' will lead them to logical definitions of 'bankrupt' and 'disrupt'.

Beck (2013) suggests an effective process for embedding new vocabulary:

- Have you heard this word before?
- Have you heard any of the parts of the word before?
- If you took the word out of the sentence, what might you replace it with to make the sentence make sense?
- Does this new word fit the rest of the extract? Might it be a synonym?
- Let's look at the meaning. Now, what's an antonym for that?
- Let's add it to our word bank and make use of both words in the future.

Take the word 'epiphany' as an example. This might be challenging, as students may not be able to relate to the word or think of other words it could be replaced with. Looking at a sentence from the authentic text *The Kite Runner* can shed some light.

> ❝I wondered if that was how forgiveness budded; not with the fanfare of epiphany, but with pain gathering its things, packing up, and slipping away unannounced in the middle of the night.❞

The context of this sentence may enable students to see that 'epiphany' links to 'fanfare' and something that is announced. They may replace it with something like 'realisation'. If you have time, you could provide another sentence using the word. For example:

> *Just when I thought I had exhausted all my ideas for the task, I had a sudden epiphany and remembered some causes of the Second World War.*

You can then do some direct vocabulary instruction and ask students to find antonyms, as outlined in Chapter 4. They could also try to use the word in their own sentences (avoid asking them to note down definitions). To consolidate their understanding of the new word and a good opposite (e.g. 'confusion') give students a creative writing task such as the one below, based on a picture stimulus.

Write a description based on this image.
Key words: epiphany, confusion

Figure 5.7: Picture stimulus and descriptive writing task

Redirecting work through metacognition

Redrafting in the 'Develop' stage requires some focus on metacognitive strategies. Metacognition is about how students survey and direct their own learning. For example, a student could assess whether a scaffold has added structure and engagement to their piece and adapt its use accordingly. Marulis & Nelson (2021) state that metacognition is a critical part of learning. The Education Endowment Foundation (EEF) agrees, arguing that metacognition supports self-regulation, which empowers students to self-assess. The EEF says that 'self-regulation is about the extent to which learners ... are aware of their strengths and weaknesses and the strategies they use to learn. It describes how they can motivate themselves to engage in learning and develop strategies to enhance their learning and to improve' (EEF, 2018). Metacognitive strategies therefore motivate students, leading to an enhancement in learning and improvement. The EEF recommends the following techniques.

- Explicitly teach metacognitive strategies such as planning, monitoring and evaluating.
- Model your own thinking.
- Set an appropriate level of challenge.
- Embed metacognitive talk.
- Teach students how to organise and manage independent learning.

A metacognition matrix like the one below can help you to implement these ideas in the classroom.

Give explicit instruction in the strategy (e.g. using talk to structure writing).	Model the strategy.	Encourage students to think about their goal; reflect on the success of a strategy towards that goal.	Make time to reflect on writing.	Include peer assessment.
Manage cognitive load.	Monitor tasks through self-assessment of the strategy.	Encourage risk-taking.	Think aloud for evaluating progress.	Use dialogic approaches to reflect on strategies.
Explicitly teach strategies for planning, revising and editing (Harris et al., 2009).	Gradually remove scaffolds so they become internalised.		Make time for self regulated independent study through spaced practice.	Complete structured reflection.

Students may be critical of the strategy for learning and want to make changes to their approach to the task. This should be encouraged as they become more independent in their learning process and how they think about that learning process.

Developing more freedom: Removing scaffolds

Once students have a good understanding of how to successfully engage a reader, you can begin to remove the scaffolds when setting tasks, to avoid them stifling creativity. This is part of the process of releasing responsibility as students start to absorb processes and recreate them instinctively. You should do this gradually, through collaborative construction of drafts in which you live-write using students' ideas. Planning is important for this:

- Think about how much of the piece of writing you will create and how much you will develop from students' responses.
- Have some planned questioning to develop student input.
- Plan how you might develop further responses (such as through discussion, cold calling or referring to a model).

To help with this type of co-writing, you could provide students with sentence starters or writing frames to support construction. Here is an example of some planned questioning when using sentence starters to support your class:

Co-written draft	Planned questioning
The air was...	How can we use some imagery to set the scene vividly?
The atmosphere radiated...	What kind of tone do we want for the piece?
The woman looked...	What sentence types will work well here?
	What adjective can you add to make that more powerful?
	How is the woman feeling? What is her objective?

Once students are confident with the features of different text types, encourage some open writing, in which they each write a piece, then swap their writing and provide feedback as the 'allied reader' for a partner. Instead of you dictating which response might work best, students can decide for themselves. In this way, you are gradually removing scaffolds as learning develops and embedding metacognition as students reflect on strategies.

Another way to gradually remove scaffolds is to replace writing frames with talk strategies to improve ideas and structure in writing. Through talk, students can rehearse their writing, and it is really useful for them to hear their piece and think like a reader, allowing them to critically reshape their first attempts. Talk can also be used as a means of peer assessment; students can give one another verbal feedback on their writing before they redraft.

The independent writer

Once you have begun to remove the scaffolds and your students are growing more confident in their understanding of audience and text type, you will see increasing independence in their writing. To enhance this, make sure that students are absolutely clear on the text type, audience and purpose of their piece, and remind them of any live modelling you have done and how this knowledge might support them.

Students will not all flourish in independent writing at the same time. Some may need one-to-one exploration of ideas first and others may need to keep their scaffolds for longer. Celebrating their successes and sharing student work in class will motivate them and consolidate knowledge about writing well.

Grammar in context

Grammar development is relevant throughout the schema from 'Define' to 'Develop'. I was educated at a time when discrete grammar had been eradicated from the curriculum, so this was the area of my teaching practice that I felt least confident about at the start. Teaching grammar discretely – that is, out of context of the curriculum – means highlighting the rules of grammatical construction without reference to the texts or themes being studied at the time. I believe the move away from discrete grammar teaching is a good thing (and I say that with a degree in Latin) because it can instil in students a rigid, rules-based understanding of language without appreciation of the stylistic choices that grammar offers. Often, grammar is unpopular because it's associated with 'correctness' and pedantic instruction, but it can be both meaningful and useful when taught in the context of texts and ideas that students are exploring and enjoying.

The following table shows some examples of discrete grammar tasks versus grammar in context.

Discrete grammar	Grammar in context
1. Highlight the personal pronouns in the following sentence: *My mother always made our dinner for us.*	*I cherished hope, it is true, but it vanished when I beheld my person reflected in water or my shadow in the moonshine, even as that frail image and that inconstant shade.* *Frankenstein*, Chapter 15
2. How is 'that' used in the following sentences? *That is my house at the end.* *Joe bought the CDs that the man was selling.*	1. How is the repetition of the pronoun in 'my person' and 'my shadow' used to emphasise the contrast between how he sees himself and how others see him? 2. How does the phrase 'even as' impact the sentence? 3. What is the effect of the demonstrative pronoun 'that'?

Grammar is interweaved with creativity. Understanding how to manipulate language through grammatical structure is an essential skill that will enable students to influence meaning and communicate knowingly, to elevate their writing and craft language in beautiful ways. Teaching grammar through authentic texts allows students to see these ideas in practice and to make informed decisions about the impact that language has.

Hancock and Kolln (2010) explain the importance of exploring and understanding metalanguage (that is, grammatical terminology) as a way of instilling social justice in the classroom. So, how do we embed this grammar teaching well?

Debra Myhill (2011) writes extensively on grammar for writing, and her studies with the University of Exeter have resulted in a number of recommendations for how it can be taught effectively:

- Use authentic examples – real texts using grammatical structures and demonstrate metalanguage through these texts.
- Make explicit links between features used and the impact they have on the reader.
- Use a process of imitation, modelling patterns used in authentic texts that students can adapt and apply to their own drafts.
- Use talk to underpin grammar for writing, exploring features and their effects dialogically.
- Encourage experimentation with language.

Based on these recommendations, it is clearly important to share a wide variety of sentence structures that students can use in their writing and to demonstrate how language can create specific effects. For example, when looking at sentence construction in the 'Compare' stage of the schema, you might explore how Keats uses subordinate clauses to have an impact on the reader in his poem 'When I have Fears that I May Cease to Be'.

> ❝ When I have fears that I may cease to be
> Before my pen has gleaned my teeming brain,
> Before high-piled books, in charactery,
> Hold like rich garners the full ripened grain;
> When I behold, upon the night's starred face,
> Huge cloudy symbols of a high romance,
> And think that I may never live to trace
> Their shadows with the magic hand of chance;
> And when I feel, fair creature of an hour,
> That I shall never look upon thee more,
> Never have relish in the faery power
> Of unreflecting love—then on the shore
> Of the wide world I stand alone, and think
> Till love and fame to nothingness do sink. ❞

The three quatrains are subordinate clauses starting with 'When' which are dependent on the main clause in the final three lines. This could be seen to evoke in the reader the same fear of an early death that Keats is expressing in the poem. Building on this, you could consider how the repetition of the word enhances the effect. Having explored these ideas as a class, you might set a poetry-writing task, asking students to use a subordinate clause with some form of repetition to have a similar impact on their reader, on the topic of something they might fear.

I find that introducing the metalanguage of grammatical constructions and terminology during the redrafting stage of writing helps to focus students' learning and equip them with the techniques needed to add flair to their writing. Discussing grammar using specific terms encourages students to think more consciously about the language they are constructing. I ensure that the emphasis is on the effects and how meaning is conveyed and not on the terminology itself, however. Writing is about choice – you don't have to use an appositive phrase for your writing to be rich and to make sense, but you can do if you wish. Our goal as teachers is to build students' ideas and to give them an armoury of approaches to shape their writing. Worrying about being 'correct' is not a state for writing, and using grammar to shape writing is something that should fill you with excitement rather than dread!

> **Reflection**
> - What grammatical structures are you confident with?
> - Do you have a good range of authentic texts you can draw on to showcase engaging structures in writing?
> - How do you currently teach grammar?
> - What might the limitations be of teaching grammar without using authentic texts?

When it comes to drafting their writing and comparing their drafts with model responses, students will find it useful to be able to isolate sentence construction. They can do this through what Myhill (2011) calls 'imitation'. Giving students concrete examples to compare with their own writing is essential to their understanding of how grammar can be adapted, such as adding detail to simple sentences. Here is an example based on a sentence from George Orwell's *Animal Farm*, showing how to add detail to simple sentences:

They all cowered in their places.
They all cowered silently in their places.
They all cowered silently in their places, seeming to know that something was about to happen.
Orwell's sentence: They all cowered silently in their places, seeming to know in advance that some terrible thing was about to happen.

Talking students through the process of adding adverbs, adjectives and clauses to a simple sentence can also support them in creating detail and enhancing effect in their own writing. Skinner (2019) shows how subordinate clauses can develop arguments; using conjunctions like 'as' and 'while' can give a sense of things happening in support of one another, while 'when' and 'if' can develop the causes of an argument.

You could provide students with a table like the one below and ask them to write a subordinate clause using each of the conjunctions, to help them apply this practice to their own writing.

Main clause (argument)	Subordinating conjunction	Subordinate clause	Final sentence
The government is wrong about cycle lanes.	As While When If Although Because While Before		For example: *Although the government is wrong about cycling lanes, they have resulted in some positive changes for the environment.*

You could ask the following questions relating to the authentic example and the table:
- Which version of the sentences is the most interesting?
- Which sentence allows us to best understand the feelings of the animals?
- Which sentence best supports the argument about cycling lanes?

Task

Using the table as a template, think of a writing task you have to teach in the next couple of weeks. Create some simple sentences that suit the task. Add some subordinate clauses for students to play around with in a comparison activity.

I recommend embedding examples from texts in your own detailed learning plan so you have authentic examples to call on to illustrate any grammar instruction; students can then consolidate and apply this knowledge themselves in their writing.

Skinner (2019) argues for an 'understanding' phase for each part of the sentence and then a 'crafting' phase, drawing on a range of different extracts, keeping grammar in context. (There is a range of wonderful lesson ideas in her teacher resource, *Crafting Brilliant Sentences*.)

In the 'Compare' stage, productive instruction can come through an examination of grammar in a descriptive sense: How does Dickens use grammar? How might that influence how I adapt my language? It is important to empower students with the idea that they have a choice – there are many different grammatical structures to try, and they should delight in the changes they can make to their language and syntax.

Try to introduce grammar teaching at a point when it is relevant to what is being learned. For example, you may be reading *A Christmas Carol* and come to the description of Fezziwig's party. Here, you could introduce students to the grammatical terms that are relevant to the extract (compound sentences, coordinating conjunctions), and support students' ability to critically engage with the text. It is imperative that grammar instruction does not turn into a feature-spotting exercise and the exploration of constructions is focused on their effect and how they construct meaning.

There were more dances, and there were forfeits, and more dances, and there was cake, and there was negus, and there was a great peice of Cold Roast, and there was a great piece of Cold Boiled, and there were mince-pies, and plenty of beer.

Fezziwig's party

Compound sentence

Connective

- Can you identify the connectives here?
- What is the impact?
- What impression does the sentence construction give of the party?

Figure 5.8: Grammar teaching based on Fezziwig's party

Here, Dickens uses a compound sentence and the repeated coordinating conjunction 'and' to give a sense of abundance and an almost overwhelming feeling of how much there is to see. You could explore this with students, giving them a different example to compare a different construction and explore the opposite impact.

Here is another example (my own!):

> ❛ Reaching about seven foot, adorned in a black, cascading cloak, clutching his bejewelled sword to his waist, he marched elegantly through the snowy forest to the clearing on the other side. ❜

Here, there are three fronted adverbials. Compare this with the simple sentence: 'He marched elegantly through the forest to the clearing on the other side.' This still makes sense – but what is lost? You could use this or another example to encourage students to consider how they might use adverbials in their own writing.

I find it useful to follow a process of purpose, application, model and discussion for grammar. It helps to consider the purpose of the sentence in order to decide on the most impactful structures. Apply this clause by clause so students can identify the discrete constructions and understand how to replicate them. Looking at a model text that is authentic or linked to the theme of the lesson will develop students' understanding of how these constructions work well in practice. You can then discuss the impact and how you might change this with different constructions. For example:

> ❝ Marching elegantly through the snowy forest, he clutched his bejewelled sword, as his black cloak cascaded from his height of seven feet and he reached the clearing on the other side. ❞

- How does having the character 'marching elegantly' first impact the reader?
- How does the use of the coordinating conjunction 'and' change the impact of the sentence?

Here is an example of this process using the description:

Purpose	Make a clear connection between what needs to be achieved and how a grammatical structure might support this.	The reader needs to be able to imagine the character, so we need a phrase or clause with some added details of their appearance.
Application	Break up the syntax for students and explore how it fulfils the purpose.	Adverbials add detail, so that readers can imagine more clearly.
Model	Explore how a writer might achieve the purpose in a model text.	Share with students the description of the character.
Discussion	Discuss how meaning is established and how different grammatical structures might change meaning.	Look at the main clause. What is the impact of reading this alone? How might you manipulate the sentence for different effects?

For me, the aim of teaching grammar is to explore the numerous possibilities of writing. During the discussion phase, it is important to emphasise creativity – using colloquial expressions, for example. Various constructions have their value and should be celebrated with your class. Of course, we do still want students' writing to make sense! To help with this, it can be useful to explore fragments that are incorrect, such as sentences missing their subject or main verb, and run-on sentences (two independent clauses that should be separated into two sentences). Understanding the ingredients of a sentence will help students to avoid these errors or to identify and fix them in the process of editing and redrafting.

Reflection

- How might you apply the process of purpose, application, model, discussion to your practice?

- Can you create some of your own sentences on a theme you are studying to showcase some grammatical structures?

- Is there an element of grammar you might need to revisit before teaching?

Case study

Sorcha (she/her), Early Career Teacher, Bloxham, Oxfordshire

With a Year 9 class in Bloxham, we were looking at this extract from *Jane Eyre*:

'Do you think, because I am poor, obscure, plain, and little, I am soulless and heartless? You think wrong! — I have as much soul as you, — and full as much heart! And if God had gifted me with some beauty and much wealth, I should have made it as hard for you to leave me, as it is now for me to leave you.'

At first teaching, we didn't explore the use of the complex sentence at the end to convey the feelings and emotions Jane has at this point. In re-teaching, I decided that a creative writing task would work well to explore her frustrations and how they are conveyed effectively in the first person. Using the metalanguage of 'complex sentence' worked well to focus student understanding. We looked at some other examples that had already been read from *Oliver Twist* and *A Midsummer Night's Dream*. Students then unpicked the feelings Jane was having when she states the above. They were able to also focus in on the use of punctuation, and we performed the speeches using some drama for reading strategies.

Collectively, we came up with success criteria for our own monologues:

- believable voice

- varied punctuation to convey emotion

- complex sentences for an exploration of Jane's determination to invert Rochester's power over her

- clarity in vocabulary.

Writing like a reader

I put the chapter on reading before the one on writing in this book to help you encourage students to write like readers. Consider Rose's (2016) structure of moving from reading to writing here (see Chapter 4). It is vital that students understand the process of reading and being captivated by a text in order to reproduce that experience for their own readers. Identifying how they feel when reading their own work during the reviewing and editing stages will give them valuable insights into how their audience is likely to respond.

The following is a process you can use to instil this approach of 'writing like a reader' in your students, as you see reading and talk as a platform and rehearsal for good writing through joint construction.

1. **Interleaving:** Include some prior knowledge of the text type through a mind map of ideas, so that students are using appropriate structures and techniques and making links between texts. Collating ideas before they write will help students to structure their material in paragraphs. Make sure the purpose of the writing is clear here.
2. **Free writing then drafting/redrafting:** Give students an opportunity to write freely, without constraints. Once they have done this and you have defined success criteria, show students the process of drafting and redrafting. This can support their understanding of where they are going with the task and will reinforce to students that their initial pieces do not need to be perfect.
3. **Compare with a model:** These examples can be at sentence level or a longer text of the type that students have to write. At the start of using this process, I would recommend using short extracts to support students' understanding of sentence-level choices.
4. **Shared reading/experiences.** Complete the process with some shared reading of what students have produced, varying the reader mode. This will give students the opportunity to be critical writers and allow them to borrow ideas from peers as well as from the models you have shared.

Strategies and takeaways

- **Lose the acronyms:** Focus on what makes English unique – developing a believable voice in writing.
- **Ideas before technicalities:** Creative ideas should always come before techniques.
- **Draft, model and think like a writer:** Focus on drafts and the idea of redrafting. Use models (but not too early) and make explicit your thought process when modelling writing to the class.
- **Develop vocabulary:** Teach root words, usable antonyms and synonyms at the same time, making sure students can transfer their use to different contexts.
- **Think metacognitively:** Improve the strategy through metacognitive activities throughout the writing process.
- **Independence is key:** Use scaffolds but remember to gradually remove them!
- **Embed the grammar:** Teach grammar in context using authentic texts.

Chapter 6: Practical application in English

Practice makes permanent

The skills and knowledge outlined in the previous chapters all combine to make English unique. In this chapter, we're going to explore how you can successfully embed these ideas and approaches in your teaching through practical application.

The classroom is an unpredictable environment and it can be difficult for new teachers to identify and use the most effective strategies in the moment (Grossman *et al*, 2009). The idea of deliberate practice – a term coined by Ericsson et al. (1993) to describe an activity that is highly structured with the specific goal of improving performance – has long been championed as a means to automate skill in teachers. They believe that deliberate practice allows teachers to isolate high-leverage changes (the actions that have the greatest impact on their practice) to rehearse them outside the classroom and then to improve their performance in the classroom through feedback from mentors.

Deliberate practice in this sense is well suited to the practical elements of classroom teaching, such as behaviour management. However, English is more nuanced than this. The highest-leverage changes discussed in Chapter 1 may apply to both in-class and out-of-class tactics. In the classroom, this might be skilful questioning to support the development of students' thinking; out of class it could be creating a scaffolded resource for writing. For this reason, I believe a better term for the mixture of behaviour, process and practice that takes place in the English classroom is 'practical application'. This covers strategies for planning, assessment, oracy, reading and writing, as well as the constant process of development and reflection required to become a really great teacher.

Mentoring

The role of mentor in schools is an important one, and it finally seems to be gaining the respect and protected time it deserves. When I first became a mentor, I was allowed time to meet with my trainee teacher but was given no guidance on how to prepare for those meetings, what to talk about, how to deliver feedback, how to practise high-leverage actions (the changes that would have the most significant impact on my mentee's practice). All these are essential, and it is important for schools to help mentors develop their skills in this way. Bambrick-Santayo and Peiser (2012) outline a six-part model for effective feedback, and it may be useful for you to understand it yourself as you work with your own mentor. This could be seen as a schema for developing practice:

1. Praise	We set the goal of X. I noticed that you X.
2. Probe	What was the purpose of X? Do you think progress happened?
3. Identify highest-leverage action step	What would be the best action step to address X?
4. Practise (or practical application)	Let's see how this might work in practice...
5. Plan ahead	When can you implement this this week?
6. Set a timeline and follow-up	When can we observe the implementation of this?

Case study

Abel, first-year trainee (he/him) and Ingrid, teacher trainer (she/her), London

Ingrid: Abel's lesson was really well sequenced using scaffolded reading, but he tended to add context before any content. He was teaching students poetry from the Renaissance, which was quite difficult, and added some group work in the hope of using effective dialogic teaching at the end. This would have been more effective if he had used it earlier, and if he had modelled and structured it for the class, so I have decided to share with him key concepts linked to different roles in group work, in the hope that he can develop his use of reciprocal reading [Palincsar and Brown, 1984]. We have talked about when this will be implemented in his lessons next week and he will follow up with his mentor and in our next observation in Term 3.

Abel: Ingrid gave me some good feedback about my lesson and I agreed the class did not have enough time to discuss any content of the poems and it was very context heavy. I know that getting them to predict, clarify, question and summarise the content first will mean they engage more with the poetry.

The power of practice

'Practice' has become a buzzword in education, but it is valuable only in the right conditions. For example, Lemov's ideas for teaching practice in *Practice Perfect* (2012) include isolating the skill to practise and making sure that the environment mimics time teaching (enacting student potential responses, for example) so that skills become automatic. These ideas are generally helpful, but they need to be adapted into subject-specific approaches (which are not always physical behaviours) when practising with mentors. To do this, it helps to first define what is a *behaviour* of an English teacher (which can be developed through practice) and what is a *process* (which can be honed through practical application). For example, behaviours (deliberate practice) include reading aloud, questioning and metacognitive modelling. Processes (practical application) might include utilising the listening matrix, preparing for an exploration of connotations with images, or preparing to explode quotations.

Developing behaviours through practice

As well as subject-specific skills, you will want to develop certain behaviours. It is useful to consider these in line with ideas about the purpose of English and the key principles we looked at in Chapter 2. In the following table, the mental model is a way of summarising the behaviour in an easy-to-remember form, which will become an automatic part of your process.

Principle	Teacher behaviour	Mental model
Collaborative experiences (construction, oracy and reading)	Think-pair-share	Set questions to allow students to think. Ensure the environment is dialogic for paired talk. Use interrogative questioning for whole-class feedback.
Modelling	Metacognitive modelling	Set expectations for the task. Think aloud changes in the model piece. Link the development of the piece to success criteria.
Targeted practice with mental models	Teacher → collaboration → student	Use the teacher → collaboration → student structure. Isolate a skill to portray/develop. Reiterate learning with a mental model.
Authentic responses and constructions	Questioning/ Collaborative modelling	Use reflective questioning to elicit personal responses. Include time for collaboration of models.
Scaffold and gradual release of responsibility	Scaffold with prompts	Set clear success criteria. Plan prompts to guide your group.
Creativity	Reading aloud	Enunciate, re-reading some passages with prosody. 'Just read' for enjoyment of the extract, inspiring creativity.
Formative feedback	Questioning	Use targeted questions to check understanding.
Peer- and self-assessment/ metacognition		Allow wait time after questions to allow students time to articulate their responses.
Questions		

Task

Identify a principle and a behaviour you would like to develop in your classroom. Decide how you will practise it. Use the table on the previous page as a model and complete the following table to help you structure your thinking. See if you can practise with your mentor.

Principle	Behaviour	Practice	Mental model

Look at this example of a deliberate practice cycle for the practical application of skills:

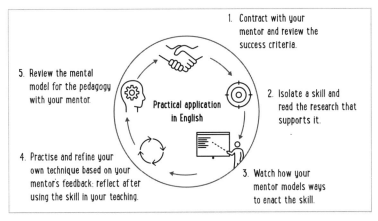

Figure 6.1: A deliberate practice cycle

The first step here is the contracting stage, in which you and your mentor agree how the practical application will work and decide what to focus on. In step 1, you should also set the success criteria. You will have already identified the highest-leverage action with your mentor after having been observed in teaching, so next they will isolate that skill and reference some research which supports its use. You might be asked to include some 'predict' activities for reading and your mentor might reference Graves and Graves' Scaffolded Reading Experience to support your understanding. It may be helpful for you to see a model that would elevate the teaching approach. Your mentor will have a relevant resource ready.

I usually adapt these resources from ones my trainees have already used. For example, perhaps they gave a creative writing task but missed out the time for students to generate their own ideas. In this case, I would use some of the same stimulus and demonstrate how to capture ideas with a scaffolded mind map. I would then ask them to apply this practically: 'Tell me how you would use it. When are you going to implement it?' You will then set an action with a definite time to follow up to see this in practice.

Concluding the application here is the 'mental model' summary. For example, you might conclude that in writing it is important to:

- model for the students
- speak aloud your thinking process
- redraft elements which need to be improved.

Repeating this three-part mental model will solidify the ideas in your mind.

The following is an example of how this might work in practice when teaching an extract from *Pride and Prejudice*. For this passage, imagine you are focusing on establishing some 'predict' reading strategies to set a focus and to ease the cognitive load of the text.

> ❛ Mr Darcy looked a little ashamed of his aunt's ill-breeding, and made no answer.
>
> When coffee was over, Colonel Fitzwilliam reminded Elizabeth of having promised to play to him; and she sat down directly to the instrument. He drew a chair near her. Lady Catherine listened to half a song, and then talked, as before, to her other nephew; till the latter walked away from her, and making with his usual deliberation towards the pianoforte stationed himself so as to command a full view of the fair performer's countenance. Elizabeth saw what he was doing, and at the first convenient pause, turned to him with an arch smile, and said:
>
> 'You mean to frighten me, Mr Darcy, by coming in all this state to hear me? I will not be alarmed though your sister does play so well. There is a stubbornness about me that never can bear to be frightened at the will of others. My courage always rises at every attempt to intimidate me.' ❜

You might use the pedagogical schema for reading from Chapter 4 to practise teaching the extract above in the following way.

Practical application	Guiding questions and information from your mentor	Notes
Contract and success criteria Have a close read of the extract that allows students to: explore Darcy's nervousness decide if Elizabeth is being honest select concrete examples from the text.	*How do you think the characters are feeling here? What do you want to convey to the students?* *We are going to look at a resource and practise this, which you will then embed into your lessons.*	
Isolate a skill and read the research Include some 'predict' reading, where you explore the characters' motivations with recall and visual exploration of ideas.	We are going to use some of the pedagogical schema for reading and include some 'predict' questions. This will allow students to make predictions about the text and help them to understand the motivations of characters when they read. What does predict do for your students?	
Watch how your mentor models the skill Use recall questions. Use visuals to collate ideas about the characters. Prep for reading with vocabulary instruction.	Recall questions you could use might be: Who is Lady Catherine? Who is Colonel Fitzwilliam? Why is Elizabeth at Rosings? Here are some visuals we could use to represent nervousness and truth. Through planned questioning we can explore what these might mean about the characters. We might zoom in on 'ill-breeding', 'stubbornness', 'pianoforte', 'intimidate' so students can comprehend the extract when they read it.	
Practise, refine and reflect Explain how the resource might support the next lesson. Practise in mentor session and give feedback linked to the contract. Set a specific goal. Reflect after teaching.	Here is the resource I would use. Adding visuals allows students to understand ideas about nervousness and honesty and about each character. Can you relay back to me why you think it is useful? Thanks for using your adapted resource in your follow-up lesson. How do you think it went? How did your students respond? Have your reflections altered in light of my feedback? How has research impacted your approach?	

Practical application	Guiding questions and information from your mentor	Notes
Review the mental model with your mentor The pedagogical schema for reading – 'predict' pre-reading (Graves and Graves, 2003) Include pre-reading to avoid cognitive overload and set a focus for the reading. Use visuals to break down concepts. Explore vocabulary to ease comprehension.	Here's the mental model for preparing to teach an extract. Can you relay it back to me in your own words? How might this process support your teaching in Language and Literature?	

Figure 6.2: A practical application guide

At first, you might find this kind of practice feels uncomfortable because you have to make yourself vulnerable in order to improve. However, your mentor should help to alleviate this through modelling and setting out expectations in the contract stage. Developing skills through this targeted approach is a route to efficiency, which should aid your motivation!

Reflection

- What is practical application?
- What preparation do you need to do to gain the most from practice?
- What additional resources could help you to achieve more efficient practice?

Isolating skills

The second step in the practical-application process involves isolating skills. In this section, we are going to delve a bit deeper into the type of skills we might want to isolate when thinking about processes beyond the classroom. Using a practical application matrix developed from the pedagogical schema for oracy, reading and writing can help you to decide what skills to isolate and what activities to use.

Practical application matrix

Oracy	Engage	Contribute	Explore	Challenge	Concur	Reflect
	Listening matrix	Talk moves	Reciprocal reading roles	Questioning Socratic circles	Balloon debate	Metacognition matrix

Reading	Predict	Respond and elaborate	Infer	Explore	Judge	
	Connotations with images	Response questions Modelling and questions beyond the text	Quotation explosions	Conscience alley drama technique	Thought-example-intent structure	

Writing	Spark	Define	Draft	Compare	Refine	Develop
	Vote with your feet Free writing	Explore success criteria	Express it better	Dismantle a model	Revise based on peer assessment	Redraft using metacognitive strategies

Some specific activities you might look at are:

- Oracy → engage → the listening matrix
- Reading → elaborate → reciprocal reading roles
- Writing → compare → dismantle a model.

From this table, we can flesh out an example for writing as:

Schema	Strategy	Research	Mental model
Writing → Develop	Redraft using metacognitive strategies	William and Marshall (2006): *Students need to be involved in the creation of success criteria.*	Students engage in issues of quality, creating their own criteria. Teacher response to their piece takes the form of questions. Students take time to read for evaluation and edit for precision.
So the focus and highest leverage change is...	The best strategy for this is...	This is based on research from... Let's looks at a resource...	To summarise the mental model is...

Here, we have selected the highest-leverage change as 'Develop', decided on a strategy and referenced some research to support this approach. The mental model summarises how this skill can become automatic.

Task

Use the grid below to plot the process for improving one of your lessons. Decide on a high-leverage change to your lesson and select a skill from the matrix to practise or apply practically with your mentor:

Practical application process to follow with your mentor		Notes
Contract and success criteria Note down the success criteria and whether you want to practice behaviour or process.		
Isolate the skill and reference the research *What skill and pedagogy are you using?*		
Model with resource (adapted from your planning) *What does your resource ask the teacher to do?*		
Practise, refine, set a goal to use in lessons, reflect after teaching Explain how the resource might support the next lesson. Practise and ask for feedback linked to the contract. Set a specific goal. Reflect after teaching using Driscoll (2007).		
Summarise a mental model for the skill and pedagogy (research) *What are the key elements of the pedagogy which can be summarised here?*		

Reflecting on progress

Throughout this book, we have encouraged reflection in a simplistic way. It is essential to reflect on your practice to assess how well you are working and to identify what you might need support with. I recommend using a model of reflection to do this, which can be especially helpful when reflecting on how to observe incidents in the classroom. One particularly good model is Brookfield's lenses (Brookfield, 1998), which give a sense of **reflexivity**. This means that in your reflection you are attentive to the social – and research-informed – origins of your own perspective and those of your students and colleagues. This gives a well-rounded view of events and allows you to remove bias and think objectively about learning incidents. I have simplified the lenses below so they can be used easily for day-to-day reflection.

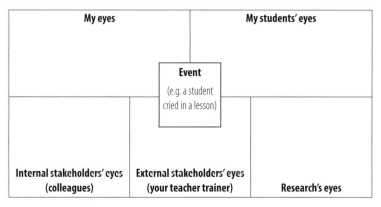

Figure 6.3: Adapted Brookfield's lenses

Another, more simplistic, reflective model to use when thinking about improving your practice as an English teacher in training is Driscoll's (2007). For example, if students are not fully comprehending a text, are not listening actively or are not able to produce something in writing, it is useful to record this as a 'feeling', then work through reason and responses using a grid like the one below.

Feeling – what?	Watching – so what?	Thinking – now what?
What happened? Who was involved? Was it good or bad?	What was the impact? Why did it happen?	What might make a positive change?
Students didn't understand the structure of the non-fiction text and did not write enough in the lesson.	They don't know how non-fiction texts are structured, so they have no examples to build on.	I need to provide some models and expose students to them through metacognitive modelling.

Task

Think of a point in your recent teaching when you experienced something like this that you can recognise as a 'feeling'. Record it in a table like the example on page 139, and decide what it shows about your students/teaching and what you can do in the future to address the issue. Deciding on the highest leverage change to your practice can help. In this example, the highest-leverage change is using metacognitive modelling.

You can follow the process for practice with your mentor to hone the skill of exposing thought process when modelling to improve students' writing. This kind of reflection will allow you to concentrate on the changes that will have the most impact.

Strategies and takeaways

- **Prioritise:** Identify where you can find the time for the practical application of processes and deliberate practice of behaviours – and prioritise it.
- **English is unique:** There are a number of English-specific skills that can be used for practical application and which can be plotted across the pedagogical schema.
- **Reflection supports your practice:** Reflect on events in your classroom using a model to identify issues, causes and plans for change.

Chapter 7: Wellbeing

Are you sitting comfortably?

English teachers regularly ask this question, especially before a story. We're keen to ensure that our students can immerse themselves in the magic of literature without being distracted by feeling uncomfortable. But does anyone check if *you* are comfortable? I once asked a leader at a school I worked at if we could get a water fountain on the first floor, and he looked at me as if I had three heads. Most days, I didn't even have time to go to the toilet, yet he thought it was reasonable for me to make it to the staffroom to get some hydration in the two minutes I had after the bell before I was missed on duty. This is just one experience that has underlined for me how important it is for teachers to feel safe, comfortable and entirely supported by their school in order to work well.

> **Reflection**
> - What provisions does your school have to make teachers comfortable?
> - Where do you do most of your work? Do you feel safe in your school environment? Why, or why not?
> - How well are your needs met as a practitioner?

Self-care

Self-care for teachers is an issue that needs to be addressed more comprehensively in many schools. When allocating time for planning and meetings, it's essential that there is a buffer for teachers that allows them to nurture their wellbeing. I remember sitting down for a feedback session during a scrutinising inspection when I was working in the Middle East. The inspector refused to start the session until I'd had a cup of tea and something to eat. It was so refreshing – after five years in the classroom I was shocked that a superior cared enough to ensure that I had time to eat! When I asked him why, he explained that he'd been shadowing me all day and had seen that I hadn't stopped. And that's the truth of it – teachers of English just don't stop. So, we need to make sure that we have time to do so, and that we feel able to discuss any individual health needs and ensure they are met with reasonable adjustments by our employers.

There are three things that you can control about your own care: thoughts, reactions and actions. Let's consider how this relates to a school context.

As teachers, many of our negative thoughts are in the first person:

- I didn't do enough planning.
- I forgot about the SEN students in that year group.
- I couldn't concentrate in the CPD session.

Changing the direction of these thoughts to focus on what the issue is can help to put things into perspective. For example, you could reframe these thoughts as follows:

- There wasn't enough time for planning. I need to speak to my mentor about my workload and strategies to plan more efficiently in the time I have.
- The information for SEN isn't clear. I need to speak to the special educational needs coordinator (SENCo) about the needs of my group, and seek training on how to adapt my planning.
- CPD was quite late in the day. I need to ensure I am fully hydrated and able to focus on the new learning. I could feed this back to my head of department.

Try to catch the thoughts before they negatively affect your perspective on the situation.

Once you have isolated the issue and identified the root cause, you can react appropriately. You can use some of the ideas at the end of Chapter 6 to help you reflect on the issue before deciding what action to take. Think about which factors lie within your **circle of control**, which lie within your **circle of influence** and which within the **circle of concern**. Remember, you can change the things that are in your circle of control, but you can only worry about the things that are in your circle of concern. For example:

- circle of control: your lessons; your planning
- circle of influence: schemes of work; departmental marking policies
- circle of concern: Ofsted early framework for reading.

Recognising the difference between these things can transform how you respond and can help to keep your worries – and your workload – in proportion.

Task

Reflect on some thoughts you have had about your work today. Plot out your reactions and then consider how you could reframe these to be positive actions. Record your ideas in a grid like this.

Thoughts	Reactions	Actions
I have a heavy workload.	I will just give up! There isn't enough time!	I'll speak to my mentor about workload and use a planning tool to help me structure my workload.

Getting wellbeing right

I suffered periods of anxiety early in my teaching career. I wasn't good at talking about it, but when I did, the suggestions people made just felt like more things to do. I was anxious because my flatmates were noisy and I wasn't sleeping; I had a Year 10 scheme of work to plan; I was being observed by a behaviour consultant with my Year 11s; I hadn't notified student loans about a change of address. When friends told me to try yoga, sit quietly in a candle-lit room, buy a facemask or have a long bath, these suggestions were just more things to add to my to-do list, increasing my anxiety.

The situation is often similar in a school context. I recently heard of a new Head of Wellbeing who was initiating a 'Friday bake', where teachers were invited to the staffroom on a Friday to have some cake. It sounds like a nice thing to do but isn't really addressing the staff's wellbeing if they've been kept at school until 6 p.m. for CPD on Wednesday and lectured in morning meetings all week about target minimum grades.

The problem with both these scenarios is that the support isn't getting to the root cause of the issue. Yoga and cake don't feel good if you don't have the space to enjoy them. Sometimes solutions are within our circle of control and we need to get to the root of the issue to see what changes we should make to have the greatest impact. Some changes are out of our control but may be within our *influence* – and its is important to make that distinction. How can you professionally guide those in leadership towards understanding what changes might have the most positive impact?

In order to properly assess what needs to change, try asking the 'five whys'.

	Eleanor at 23	**Staff at school**
	Feels anxious/can't sleep well.	**Feel undervalued**/ill-humoured at work/ want to move schools.
Why?	Hasn't eaten properly this week.	Constant deadlines emailed out.
	Has an overwhelming workload.	Meetings every evening for different training.

	Eleanor at 23	**Staff at school**
Why?	Doesn't have time to shop. Behaviour is bad in Year 11 so consultant is adding pressure.	SLT under pressure to reach targets set by head.
Why?	Is working 7 a.m. to 7 p.m. Routines not in place. SLT keen on silent lessons.	School failed last inspection.
Why?	Works in a highly pressured environment with lack of motivation, and home is not relaxing.	Staff are unhappy and not performing at their best, affecting students' results.
Why?	Too much pressure from different sources. Boundaries not in place at home.	Leadership do not show they value staff. Too many responsibilities placed on staff.
Solutions	Professional: Eradicate pressure by exploring options with mentor for fewer observations and reducing workload. Personal: Set boundaries to ensure time for relaxing and rejuvenating is protected. Decide on goals.	Professional: Value workforce by giving them the freedom to make decisions about their practice. Personal: Give staff time by eradicating erroneous tasks.

Task

Identify a situation that is causing you anxiety. Using a table like the one above, try the 'five whys' to get to the root of the issue and find a solution.

I really struggled to eradicate the pressure myself. A professional solution was needed and I required input from leadership to support me in this change. If you're experiencing a difficult situation in your professional life, try turning to support networks within your school and any that you may find through your training provider or union.

Reflection

- If you had all the time in the world, what would you do to make yourself feel good?
- What helps you relax?
- Are the basics right? Are you drinking enough water? Sleeping? Eating a balanced diet?
- If there are no basics in place, what factors in your circle of control should you change?

The wellbeing wheel

To survive all the pressures of life, in and out of the classroom, it's essential to prioritise your own wellbeing. This is a very personal thing – I love yoga, for example, but it's not everyone's cup of tea! Decide what *you* need to ensure that you feel mentally strong and physically nourished.

There are several aspects of wellbeing that it may help to focus on as an English teacher.

Figure 7.1: The wellbeing wheel (adapted from CBSH Health, 'The Wellbeing Wheel')

Reflection

- It's helpful to start with occupational wellbeing.
- Why are you a teacher? What made you train?
- If the DfE, Ofsted and your SLT didn't exist, how would you imagine your classroom?
- What can you conceivably do to create the climate you would like to see?

Task

Look at each aspect on the wheel in turn. Answer the questions for each aspect to assess how they influence your own life. Try to identify areas that need to change to make you happier in your job and life. Finally, rank each aspect of your wellbeing in order of importance.

Aspect of wellbeing	Reflection	Rank 1–8
Social	What social connections do you have at work? What support do you have outside of work?	
Emotional	How emotional do you feel at work? Are you able to process difficult situations that arise? Is there support?	
Spiritual	How spiritual are you? Do you find spiritual guidance at school supportive?	
Intellectual	Do you have time to enhance your subject knowledge? What intellectual gaps would you like to address?	
Physical	What is your physical health like? Do you exercise regularly? What might you change about this?	
Climate	Where do you work? What space do you have to do your planning? Do you take work home? Is this conducive to focus and relaxation?	
Job role	Are you happy in your current position? What are your aspirations? Do you have enough support to get there?	
Financial	How are your finances? Can you save? Can you afford to look after yourself?	

Making changes

What specific changes can you make to improve your wellbeing as a teacher?

1. Easy, nutritious food

It is essential to get the basics right! Here are some ideas from my mother – who has worked in catering for over 40 years – for ways you can add more nutrition to your day.

Breakfast ideas	Easy lunches	Batch-cooked dinners	Snacks for meetings
Overnight oats, banana bread, blueberry muffins, porridge with berries and honey, almond butter protein smoothie	Salmon and buckwheat noodles, poke bowl, humus and fritters	Vegan Bolognese; fish pie; harissa salmon/vegetable traybake; chicken, tomato and olive traybake	Flapjacks, oat biscuits, almond butter cookies

2. Build in reflection to identify your priorities

Journalling can really help you capture and clarify your thoughts, and can stop you feeling overwhelmed, as all those worries and tasks can live on paper rather than in your head. When you wake up in the night and can't stop thinking about an email you must send, write it down. Don't send it, just remind yourself to do it. It is also useful to prioritise your to-do list. The Eisenhower decision matrix (McKay and McKay, 2013) can help you to plan your top priorities and ensure you have space in your life for everything that is important to you. Try using the adapted version of the matrix below.

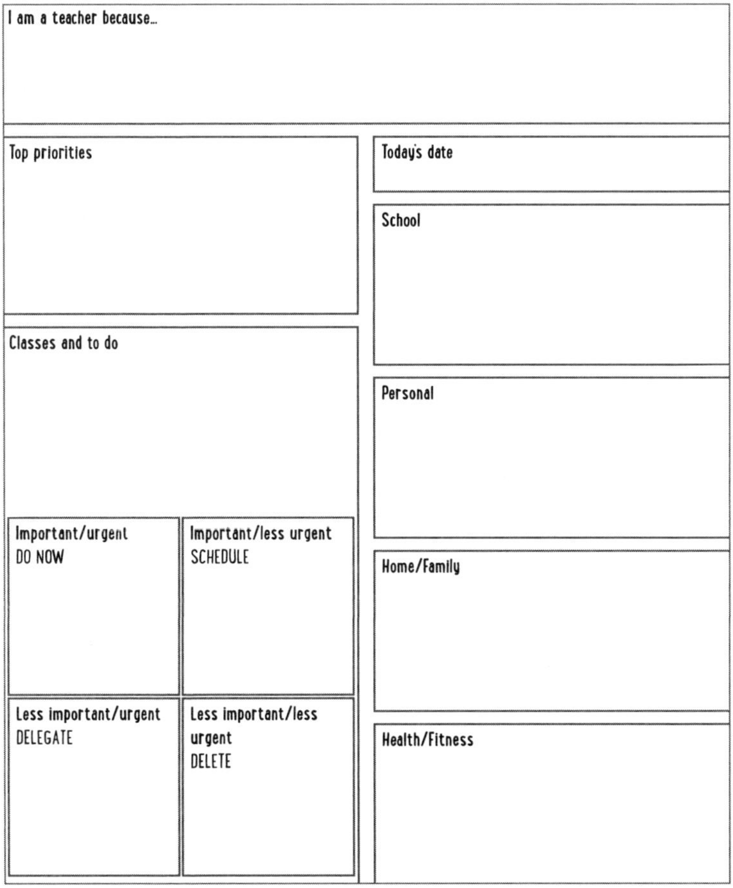

Figure 7.2: Adapted Eisenhower matrix

Start by reflecting on why you became a teacher. Then set a focus for your intentions for the day – what motivates you (this may change daily). Complete your 'to do' list for school, personal, home/family and health/fitness. Use the matrix to prioritise what is urgent and to deprioritise what might be extraneous tasks. Going to the gym might be urgent, re-doing a presentation with new images may be an unnecessary task, taking up time unnecessarily. Decide on your top priorities, thinking about your own well-being, and summarise these on the left-hand side.

> **Task**
>
> Copy and complete the template in Figure 7.2 for your day ahead. Try making this a habit for the next two months and see what impact it has on your teaching practice – and life in general.

3. Time-saving teacher hacks

Here are some suggestions for ways you can save time and make your life easier.

Live mark: This is better for your workload as well as being better for your students. They get instant feedback, they don't have to spend hours deciphering terrible handwriting, and they can action it straight away. I am a big fan of 'big write' lessons at the end of the week – set aside time for extended writing, where you circulate the room and live mark, giving students timely feedback.

Create codes for popular marking targets: Put the code in books instead of writing it all out – ensure you ask questions to make it responsive.

Adapt other resources: Use and adapt resources produced by expert teachers to inspire you, then try making your bespoke materials for your classes.

Get to know data and use Excel: Familiarise yourself with the data processes for your institution and import your data into Excel. Keep track of students easily through spreadsheets for each group, which you can use to make seating plans and group roles prior to lessons.

Use a timer: Add pace to your classes and ensure you cover content by timing activities and transitions. Have the clock visible so students are on board. This sets them up well for exams and also establishes skills of efficiency for the world of work.

Use the technology available at your school: Have an online homework tracker at school? Get used to using it and making it work for your class. Use it to log behaviour – and remember to log praise as much as you can. This will please the SLT, who may have invested a lot in IT programs, and it will make your life easier too!

Get the class to create a set of questions they can ask themselves when annotating, analysing or evaluating texts: These can be saved somewhere on a PowerPoint slide or made into a wall display, so you don't need to keep typing things out, and there is a set that classes are 'trained' to use.

4. Have morning and evening rituals

Make time in the morning for rituals that make you ready for the day ahead. Wake up early. Make your bed. Have some time alone with some hot water and lemon meditating on what's to come or just freeing your mind of all thought. Take a walk in nature if you can. Recite some affirmations: I am a great teacher; I am confident and bright. Think about carving out some time in the evening for rituals too. Prepare yourself for the next day by noting down your goals in a journal. Reflect on what you have achieved and what's gone well in your English lessons. Using Driscoll's (2007) reflective model can help here. Clear your head with some light reading (something you're not teaching) to nourish your soul. Make sure you have a good sleep routine in place and go to bed at the same time every night, minimising the use of your phone just before bed.

Try mapping out an ideal morning and evening routine, note down all the rituals you would like to do and pick the ones that are most realistic. Stay flexible and keep adjusting your routine, but track your progress in a journal to see the impact on your day-to-day life.

Holidays

We all have those annoying friends who think that teachers have it easy. 'Look at your holidays! You get loads of time off.' Throughout my years of teaching, I've realised that the only time off teachers really get is in the summer. Other breaks are filled with revision sessions, mock marking, planning for the next term, and so on. You're lucky if you get a couple of days off, and even then your mind is so full of work you don't always fully switch off. To address this, make sure you block out some time in your holidays that's just for you. Keep the first part of half-term week as free time and book something to do with friends or family. If you don't start working until Thursday, it can only run into Friday and not the entire week! Timetable your workload and have realistic aims.

Unfortunately, I don't know a teacher who doesn't work at the weekend, but after a few years in the classroom I managed to have some weekends off and now I only do a couple of hours on a Sunday. Be strict with yourself and make your boundaries clear. Don't be afraid to set your own limits and stick to them. When you work hard in the week, a compromise can always be found. To protect your time off, try and make your phone solely for pleasure: delete any work-related apps or silence the notifications. Time off to reconnect with who you are beyond the classroom is essential, and will make you a much better teacher.

Research has found that a habit takes 66 days to become automatic, so make a plan for the next two months for the habits you'd like to embed into your practice.

Morning meditation for teachers

All this can be very time-consuming, so you will need to free up time and space in your mind. Mindfulness and meditation can be useful for this, so I'm going to leave you with a literary-inspired meditation that you can do every morning. You could record the script to play to yourself.

Time: 10 minutes

It is essential to clear the obstacles for this morning meditation, so start by finding somewhere comfortable to sit, away from any distractions. Take some time to breathe deeply: a strong inhalation, hold your breath for four seconds and exhale slowly through the mouth for four seconds. Repeat for three breaths and on the third, start to close your eyes.

You may be thinking now, 'I don't have time.' Catch this as a thought and observe it. Repeat to yourself: 'I have the time to nurture my wellbeing.' Keep breathing deeply and start to do a body scan. How is the head feeling? Relax the eyes, the nose, the mouth. Relax all the muscles in the neck, the shoulders, the torso, feel yourself relax the gut. Relax the legs and feel the muscles in the feet melt into the floor. Keep breathing deeply and count your breaths. Enjoy the feeling of switching off.

You may start thinking about the lessons you have today. Catch those thoughts, observe them and focus back on the breath. You might feel like you can't sit still; if so, consider changing this to a walking meditation tomorrow, keeping the eyes in soft focus and relaxing as much as you can when you walk.

Keep those steady breaths and set an intention for today. What is it you'd like to achieve? Think of one personal goal and one professional aim. Hold these in your mind and repeat them.

Now it's time for some joy. You can change this poem each day. Repeat to yourself the lines:

> Love's not Time's fool, though rosy lips and cheeks
> Within his bending sickle's compass come;
> Love alters not with his brief hours and weeks,
> But bears it out even to the edge of doom.
> If this be error and upon me prov'd,
> I never writ, nor no man ever lov'd.

What is it you love about yourself? What do you love about your job? Repeat this and hold it in your mind throughout the day.

Shift your expectations now from thinking or doing to being. Be that teacher who students never forget. Inject the heart into pedagogy.

Strategies and takeaways

- **Think about what you love about learning:** The mind is such a wonderful thing and as teachers we are privileged to use ours to influence others' learning every day. How can you use your knowledge about how we learn to help others?
- **Reflect on what you have learned about pedagogy:** How do the schemas mean you can inject some heart into your teaching practice?
- **Think about oracy in your classroom:** How passionate do you feel about encouraging the next generation of confident communicators? How can you bring some love into listening and talk in your classroom?
- **Reflect on your practice of reading:** How do you convey your passion for reading to your class, exploring new genres, engaging with poetry, and bringing drama to the classroom?
- **Think about the power of writing:** That ability you have to express yourself in words and craft language is so precious. How can you bring that ardent idea to your class and allow them to realise the power of their own syntax?
- **Finally, how can you bring all this together through practical application?** How can you translate that love of our incredible subject to the classroom? What makes English unique and how can you practise those distinct skills?

References and further reading

Chapter 1

Adey, P. and Shayer, M. (2015). 'The Effects of Cognitive Acceleration'. Available at: https://www.letsthinkinenglish.org/wp-content/uploads/2012/06/TheEffectsofCognitiveAcceleration.pdf

Education Endowment Foundation (EEF, 2021). 'Cognitive Science Approaches In The Classroom: A Review Of The Evidence'. Available at: https://d2tic4wvo1iusb.cloudfront.net/documents/guidance/Cognitive_science_approaches_in_the_classroom_-_A_review_of_the_evidence.pdf?v=1629124457

Elbow, P. (1995). *Peter Elbow on Writing: A Conversation With America's Top Writing Teacher*. Media Education Foundation.

Gibbons, P. (2002). *Scaffolding Language, Scaffolding Learning*. London: Heinemann.

Graves, M. and Graves, B. (2003). 'Scaffolding Reading Experiences: Designs for Student Success'. Second Edition.

Hayes, J.R. (2006). 'New Directions in Writing Theory' in C.A. MacArthur, S. Graham, and J. Fitzgerald (Eds), *Handbook of Writing Research* (pp. 28–40). New York: The Guilford Press.

Lemov, D. (2021). *Teach Like a Champion 3.0: 63 Techniques that Put Students on the Path to College*. San Francisco: Jossey-Bass

Mercer, N. (2008). 'Classroom dialogue and the teacher's role' in *Education Review*, 21(1), pp. 60–65. Available at: https://educationpublishing.com/wp-content/uploads/2019/06/Education_Review_Vol.21_No.1.pdf#page=66

Rose, D. (2016). 'Engaging and supporting all our students to read and learn from reading', PETAA Paper Vol. 202.

Shulman, L. (1986). 'Those Who Understand: Knowledge Growth in Teaching', in *Educational Researcher* (15:2), pp. 4–14.

Willingham, D.T. (2009). *Why don't students like school? A cognitive scientist answers questions about how the mind works and what it means for the classroom*. San Francisco: Jossey-Bass.

Chapter 2

Cremin, T. and Myhill, D. (2012). *Writing Voices: Creating Communities of Writers* (Chapter 2). London: Routledge.

Eggen, P. and Kauchak, D. (2001). *Educational Psychology: Classroom Connections*. 5th Edition. New York: Macmillan.

Marshall, B. and Wiliam, D. (2006). *English Inside the Black Box*. London: NFER.

Muijs, D. and Reynolds, D. (2011). *Effective Teaching: Evidence and Practice*. 3rd Edition. Los Angels, CA: Sage.

Palincsar, A.S. and Brown, A.L. (1984). 'Reciprocal Teaching of Comprehension: Fostering and Comprehension Monitoring Activities', *Cognition and Instruction*, 1(2) pp. 117–75, Lawrence Erlbaum Associates, Inc.

Rosen, M. (2017). 'For teachers: how to assess and analyse ways in which pupils respond to stories, poems and plays' (blog post). Available at: https://michael-rosenblog.blogspot.com/2017/04/for-teachers-how-to-assess-and-analyse.html

Spires, H. and Stone. D. (1989). 'The Directed Notetaking Activity: A Self-Questioning Approach', in *Journal of Reading* (33:1), pp. 36–39.

Willingham, D.T. (2019). 'How to Teach Critical Thinking: A paper commissioned by the NSW Department of Education'. Available at: http://www.danielwillingham.com/uploads/5/0/0/7/5007325/willingham_2019_nsw_critical_thinking2.pdf

Chapter 3

Alexander, R. (2020). *A Dialogic Teaching Companion*. London: Routledge.

AQA (2022). 'Worlds and Lives' cluster in *Poems Past and Present*.

Cambridge University Press & Assessment (2022). *Education brief: Oracy* (2022). Available at: https://www.cambridgeinternational.org/Images/661428-education-brief-oracy-.pdf

Education Endowment Foundation (EEF, 2021). 'Teaching and Learning Toolkit: Oral language interventions'. Available at: https://educationendowmentfoundation.org.uk/education-evidence/teaching-learning-toolkit/oral-language-interventions

Mercer, N. (2008). 'Classroom dialogue and the teacher's role', *Education Review*, 21, 1, 60-65. Available at: https://educationpublishing.com/wp-content/uploads/2019/06/Education_Review_Vol.21_No.1.pdf#page=66

Mercer, N. (2008). 'Five examples of talk in groups'. Available at: https://thinkingtogether.educ.cam.ac.uk/resources/5_examples_of_talk_in_groups.pdf

Northcott, Kerri (2023). 'My daughter's a social media star – I have no regrets', *The Sunday Times*, 12 March 2023. Available at: https://www.thetimes.co.uk/article/my-daughters-a-social-media-star-and-i-have-no-regrets-spsqklf8s.

Oracy Cambridge and Voice 21's Oracy Framework (2020). Available at: https://voice21.org/wp-content/uploads/2022/09/The-Oracy-Framework-2021-1-1.pdf and https://oracycambridge.org/wp-content/uploads/2020/06/The-Oracy-Skills-Framework-and-Glossary.pdf

National Literacy Trust (NLT, 2012). 'Understanding different types of talk'. Available at: https://literacytrust.org.uk/resources/understanding-teaching-talk-secondary-classroom/

Palincsar, A.S. and Brown, A.L. (1984). 'Reciprocal Teaching of Comprehension: Fostering and Comprehension Monitoring Activities', *Cognition and Instruction*, 1(2) pp. 117–75, Lawrence Erlbaum Associates, Inc.

Chapter 4

Al-Jamri, A., Benjamin-Lewis, J., Bhavsar, P. et al. (2021). *Who We Are: 24 brilliant texts to enrich your KS3 English curriculum* (KS3 anthology pack). London: HarperCollins.

Appleyard, J.A. (1991). *Becoming a Reader: The Experience of Fiction from Childhood to Adulthood*. Cambridge: Cambridge University Press.

AQA GCSE English Literature, Paper 2: Shakespeare and unseen poetry, November 2021.

AQA GCSE English Literature, Shakespeare and Unseen Poetry, Report on the Examination, November 2021.

AQA (2022). 'Worlds and Lives' cluster in *Poems Past and Present*.

Cremin, T. (2020). 'Reading for Pleasure: challenges and opportunities', in Davison, J. and Daly, C. (Eds), *Debates in English Teaching. Debates in Subject Teaching*. London: Routledge.

Curtis, C. (2022). *Develop Brilliant Reading: KS3 Teacher Pack*. London: HarperCollins.

Department for Education. (May 2012). 'Research evidence on reading for pleasure', Education standards research team. Available at: https://assets.publishing.service.gov.uk/government/uploads/system/uploads/attachment_data/file/284286/reading_for_pleasure.pdf

Frayer, D., Frederick, W.C. and Klausmeier, H.J. (1969) *A Schema for Testing the Level of Cognitive Mastery*. Madison, WI: Wisconsin Center for Education Research.

Friere, P (1985). 'Reading the World and Reading the Word: An Interview with Paulo Freire'. *Language Arts* (62:1), pp.15–21.

Graves, M. and Graves, B. (2003). 'Scaffolding Reading Experiences: Designs for Student Success'. Second Edition.

Kispal, A. (2008). 'Effective Teaching of Inference Skills for Reading'. Literature Review, Department for Children, Schools and Families, National Foundation for Educational Research 2008. Available at: https://www.nfer.ac.uk/publications/edr01/edr01.pdf

Lunzer, G., and Gardner, K. (1984). *Learning from the Written Word*. London: Heinemann.

McGeown et al. (2016), 'Understanding children's reading activities: Reading motivation, skill and child characteristics as predictors'. *Journal of Research in Reading* (39:1), pp. 109–125.

OECD (2019). 'PISA 2018 Reading Framework'. Available at: https://www.oecd-ilibrary.org/docserver/5c07e4f1-en.pdf?expires=1694686747&tid=id&tac-cname=guest&checksum=58664FB8B6CD8506909359CEF2A50883.

Ofsted's framework for early reading. (July 2023). Available at: https://assets.publishing.service.gov.uk/government/uploads/system/uploads/attachment_data/file/1178136/The_Reading_Framework_2023.pdf

Oliver, K. (2017). 'PEE? PEAL? PETAL?', English and Media Centre. Available at: https://www.englishandmedia.co.uk/blog/pee-peal-petal

Palincsar, A.S. and Brown, A.L. (1984). 'Reciprocal Teaching of Comprehension: Fostering and Comprehension Monitoring Activities', *Cognition and Instruction*, 1(2) pp. 117–75, Lawrence Erlbaum Associates, Inc.

Rose, D. (2016). 'Engaging and supporting all our students to read and learn from reading'. PETAA PAPER. 202. 1–12. Available at: https://www.researchgate.net/publication/321996105_Engaging_and_supporting_all_our_students_to_read_and_learn_from_reading

Smith, H. and Lander, V. (2023). 'Anti-racism framework for Initial Teacher Education/Training'. Newcastle University. Available at: https://www.ncl.ac.uk/mediav8/institute-for-social-science/files/Global%20Literature%20review%20-%20final.pdf

The National Literacy Trust (2023). 'Children's and young people's reading in 2023', Available at: https://literacytrust.org.uk/research-services/research-reports/children-and-young-peoples-reading-in-2023/

Westbrook et al. (2018). '"Just reading": the impact of a faster pace of reading narratives on the comprehension of poorer adolescent readers in English classrooms: Reading narratives at a faster pace. University of Sussex.

Zwaan, R.A. and Radvansky, G.A. (1998). 'Situation models in language comprehension and memory'. *Psychological Bulletin*, 123(2), pp. 162–185. Available at: https://doi.org/10.1037/0033-2909.123.2.162.

Chapter 5

AQA GCSE English Language Paper 1, Examiner Report 2021

Beck, I. (2013). *Bringing words to life: Robust vocabulary instruction.* London: The Guildford Press.

Corbett, P. and Strong, J. (2021). *Talk for Writing Across the Curriculum: How to teach non-fiction writing to 5–12 year-olds.* London: McGraw Hill.

EEF. Metacognitions and self regulation report. Available at: https://educationendowmentfoundation.org.uk/education-evidence/guidance-reports/metacognition

Elbow, P. (1973). *Writing Without Teachers.* New York: Oxford University Press.

Elbow, P. (2000). *Everyone Can Write: Essays Toward Hopeful Theory of Writing and Teaching Writing.* Oxford: Oxford University Press.

Gibbons, P. (2002). *Scaffolding Language, Scaffolding Learning.* London: Heinemann.

Halliday, M.A.K. and Martin, J.R. (Eds) (1993). *Writing Science: Literacy and Discursive Power.* Bristol/London: The Falmer Press.

Hancock, C. and Kolln, M. (2010). *Blowin' in the Wind: English Grammar in United States Schools.* New York: Routledge.

Harris, K., Santangelo, T. and Graham, S. 'Metacognition and Strategies Instruction in Writing', in Salatas Waters. H. and Schneider, W. (Eds) (2009) *Metacognition, Strategy Use, and Instruction.* New York: Guilford Press.

Hayes, J.R. (2006), 'New directions in writing theory', in C. MacArthur, S. Graham, and J. Fitzgerald (Eds), *Handbook of Writing Research*, pp. 28–40, New York: Guilford.

Marshall, B. and Wiliam, D. (2006). *English Inside the Black Box.* London: NFER.

Marulis, L.M. and Nelson, L.J. (2021). 'Metacognitive processes and associations to executive function and motivation during a problem-solving task in 3–5-year-olds'. *Metacognition and Learning*, 16(1), pp. 207–231.

Myhill, D., Lines, H. and Watson A. (2011). 'Making Meaning with Grammar: A repertoire of possibilities', *mETAphor*, Issue 2.

Rose, D. (2016). 'Engaging and supporting all our students to read and learn from reading'. PETAA PAPER. 202. 1-12. Available at: https://www.researchgate.net/publication/321996105_Engaging_and_supporting_all_our_students_to_read_and_learn_from_reading

Rose, D. and Martin, J.R. (2012). *Learning to Write, Reading to Learn: Genre, Knowledge and Pedagogy in the Sydney School.* Sheffield: Equinox Publishing.

Skinner, L. (2019). *Crafting Brilliant Sentences.* London: HarperCollins.

Chapter 6

Bambrick-Santoyo, P. and Peiser, B.M. (2012). *Leverage leadership: A practical guide to building exceptional schools.* San Francisco: Jossey-Bass.

Brookfield, S. (1998). 'Critically Reflective Practice', in *The Journal of Continuing Education in the Health Professions,* Volume 18, pp. 197–205.

Driscoll, J.J. (2007). 'Supported reflective learning: the essence of clinical supervision?' in *Practising Clinical Supervision: A Reflective Approach for Healthcare Professionals* (2nd edition), pp. 27–50. London: Bailliere Tindall.

Ericsson, K. A., Krampe, R.T. and Tesch-Römer, C. (1993). 'The role of deliberate practice in the acquisition of expert performance', in *Psychological Review,* 100(3), pp. 363–406.

Grossman, P. *et al.* (2009). 'Teaching Practice: A Cross-Professional Perspective', in *Teachers College Record,* 111(9), pp. 2055–2100. Available at: https://tedd.org/wp-content/uploads/2014/03/Grossman-et-al-Teaching-Practice-A-Cross-Professional-Perspective-copy.pdf

Lemov, D. (2012). *Practice Perfect: 42 Rules for Getting Better at Getting Better.* San Francisco: Jossey Bass.

Palincsar, A.S. and Brown, A.L. (1984). 'Reciprocal Teaching of Comprehension: Fostering and Comprehension Monitoring Activities', *Cognition and Instruction,* 1(2) pp. 117–75, Lawrence Erlbaum Associates, Inc.

Chapter 7

CBHS Health. (2020). 'The Wellbeing Wheel'. https://www.cbhs.com.au/mind-and-body/blog/the-wellbeing-wheel

Driscoll, J.J. (2007). 'Supported reflective learning: the essence of clinical supervision?' in *Practising Clinical Supervision: A Reflective Approach for Healthcare Professionals* (2nd edition), pp. 27–50. London: Bailliere Tindall.

McKay, B. and McKay, K. (2013). 'The Eisenhower Decision Matrix: How to Distinguish Between Urgent and Important Tasks and Make Real Progress in Your Life', in *A Man's Life, Personal Development.* Archived from the original on 2014-03-22. Retrieved 2014-03-22.

Glossary

circle of concern – anything that affects you or that you care about but do not have direct power to change (the weather; politics)

circle of control – anything that can be affected by actions that come specifically from you (thoughts, behaviours, responses, attitudes)

circle of influence – anything that can be affected by the actions of others but over which you have some impact (e.g. team morale)

cognitive conflict – being presented with a different viewpoint, interpretation or set of evidence that contradicts a person's current viewpoint, opening up an opportunity to develop their thinking

declarative knowledge – knowledge that focuses on the 'what'; facts and information about a topic (e.g. timelines and vocabulary)

deliberate practice – purposeful and systematic repetition of skills with feedback to develop automaticity of a new skill

dialogic – describing things relating to dialogue; dialogic teaching is where students' thinking is enhanced through questions designed to encourage extension, discussion and reasoning, and to prompt debate about a topic

didactic – teaching through telling; when a teacher tells students new information rather than students discussing or finding it out experientially

formative assessment – the process of continuous assessment during teaching, through monitoring and feedback

free writing – a technique to encourage creativity that involves writing ideas continuously without worrying about form or structure

interleaving – a teaching process in which students learn different concepts and practise different skills in combination, to strengthen their understanding and retention, and to help them transfer their knowledge and skills to new contexts

mental model – an internal representation of an external idea, or an explanation of how something fits together; a concept or framework that helps to shape behaviour and approaches to problem-solving

metacognition – an awareness and understanding of one's own thought processes

non-declarative knowledge – knowledge that is not dependent on facts and that supports skills and habits, such as procedural knowledge

oracy – the skills of listening and expressing oneself fluently in speech

reasoning – the cognitive process of making sense of information, drawing conclusions and forming evaluations based on evidence and logic; reasoning requires critical thinking

reciprocal reading strategies – using the roles of predictor, clarifier, questioner and summariser to scaffold reading

reflexivity – the fact of being able to examine your own feelings, motives and behaviours

retrieval practice – the practice of bringing previously learned material to mind, strengthening memory and making it easier for ideas to be recalled in the future

Socratic circle – a central circle of students asking questions of the text; an outer circle of students listening and evaluating

spaced practice – a process in which students review and revisit material over a long period of time, developing connections between ideas

Dedication

This book came to life in Papillon, Liverpool. Since that initial conversation with some notes on a napkin, it has grown beautiful wings and flown majestically from its cocoon along with its wonderful companion *Curriculum with Soul*. Thank you to Jo Heathcote for that lunch and for believing in me. Huge thanks to the entire subject expert team for being such inspiring guides and for their support. Thank you also to all my students, who have taught me more than I have taught them.

Thank you also to my wonderful mum for setting me this challenge and cooking me feasts after days of writing and to Georgie for helping me define pedagogy on a memorable ramble. My biggest thanks goes to someone who can't hear it. You always told me I should write a book Dad – if only you could read this one. This is for you.

Acknowledgements

Texts and diagrams

We are grateful to the following for permission to reproduce copyright material:

Extracts on pp.38–39 adapted from 'For teachers: how to assess and analyse ways in which pupils respond to stories, poems and plays' by Michael Rosen, https://michaelrosenblog. blogspot.com/2017/04/for-teachers-how-to-assess-and-analyse.html, copyright © Michael Rosen, 2017; Diagram on p.53 adapted from *A Dialogic Teaching Companion* by Robin Alexander, Taylor & Francis, copyright © 2020. Reproduced by permission of Taylor and Francis Group, LLC, a division of Informa plc.; Extract on p.61 from 'Research evidence on reading for pleasure, Education standards research team', May 2012, p.9, Department of Education, © Crown copyright 2012, under the terms of the Open Government Licence v2.0.; Poem on p.81 "Homing" by Liz Berry from *Black Country* by Liz Berry, Chatto and Windus, copyright © Liz Berry, 2014. Reprinted by permission of The Random House Group Limited; Extracts on pp.82, 83 and 98 from 'AQA GCSE English Literature question paper, Paper 2: Shakespeare and unseen poetry', November 2021, p.6; 'AQA GCSE English Literature, Shakespeare and Unseen Poetry, Report on the Examination', November 2021, p.5; and 'AQA GCSE English Language Examiner's Report', Paper 1, 2021. AQA material is reproduced by permission of AQA; Table on p.114 adapted from *Everyone Can Write: Essays Toward Hopeful Theory of Writing and Teaching Writing* by Peter Elbow, Oxford University Press, 2000, p.29, copyright © Peter Elbow, 2000. Reproduced with permission of the Licensor through PLSClear; Summary of Seven recommendations on p.118 from "Improving Literacy in Secondary Schools: Guidance Report" Education Endowment Foundation, July 2018, https:// educationendowmentfoundation.org.uk/education-evidence/guidance-reports/literacy-ks3-ks4, © Crown copyright.; and a table on p.130 from *Leverage leadership: A Practical Guide to Building Exceptional Schools* by Paul Bambrick-Santoyo & Brett M. Peiser, Jossey-Bass, 2012, copyright © John Wiley & sons, Inc., 2012. All rights reserved.

Images

p.7 AnnaStills/Shutterstock; p.20 EF Stock/Shutterstock; p.24 Duncan Andison/Shutterstock; p.30 Jacob Lund/Shutterstock; p.34 EF Stock/Shutterstock; p.35 studiovin/Shutterstock; p.41 EF Stock/Shutterstock; p.49 stock_photo_world/Shutterstock; p.45tl Klahan/Shutterstock; p.45cl Dr.OGA/Shutterstock; p.45cr Kanea/Shutterstock; p.45bc SvetaZi/Shutterstock; pp.50, 51 jointstar/Shutterstock, p.52 as-artmedia/shutterstock; p.62 George Dolgikh/ Shutterstock; p.65 DGLimages/Shutterstock; p.66bl salajean/Shutterstock; p.66br Darren Baker/Shutterstock; p.66tr Harish Marnad/Shutterstock; p.67tl Premium Art/Shutterstock; p.67tr 4LUCK/Shutterstock; p.67m Kengi/Shutterstock; p.67bl Olena Go/Shutterstock; p.67br Elena100/Shutterstock; p.68bl John Cairns/Shutterstock; p.68cr WICHAI WONGJONGJAIHAN/ Shutterstock; p.68tl tomertu/Shutterstock; p.77 Volodymyr Martyniuk/Shutterstock; p.78 michel arnault/Shutterstock; p.84tr Kurit afshen/Shutterstock; p.84tl Jakub Krechowicz/ Shutterstock; p.84cr FotoMikv/Shutterstock; p.84cl MDL80/Shutterstock; p.84cr Janick C/ Shutterstock; p.84cl MDL80/Shutterstock; p.84cr Janick C/Shutterstock; p.84br Darren Baker/ Shutterstock; p.87 5 second Studio/Shutterstock; p.92 kashidi/Shutterstock; p.108 PopTika/ Shutterstock; p.111 phaustov/Shutterstock; p.117 Sergey Nesterchuk/Shutterstock; p.124 VTT Studio/Shutterstock; p.127 Monkey Business Images/Shutterstock; p.130 Ground Picture/ Shutterstock; p.131 Gorodenkoff/Shutterstock; p.145 fizkes/Shutterstock